A sweet friendship refreshes the soul.
—Proverbs 27:9b The Message

This book is dedicated to my better half of over three decades, and my best friend, John Garnett Hoagland, Senior. His relentless support has been simultaneously sweet and nothing short of miraculous. I'm beyond blessed the Lord intersected our path on the pier in Naples, Florida, in 1981, later blessing us with a full quiver of three sons, three daughters-in-love, and one very pink granddaughter (with more grandbabies on the way). To God be the glory.

Contents

Foreword

Before you embark on this delightful road trip with my forever friend, Elizabeth Hoagland, you need to know three important things about her.

First, she really *does* have this many close friends. Around the fifth chapter, you're going to start shaking your head, thinking, *No way can one woman maintain all these meaningful friendships.* I promise you, Elizabeth faithfully takes the time—or *makes* the time—to keep each relationship humming along at a happy pace.

Elizabeth cultivates her friendships like a gardener tends her flowers: watering them with care, dispensing with any weeds before they take root, and feeding each plant regularly. *Very* regularly.

Which brings me to the second important thing. This woman loves food. I mean, she *loves* food. She knows the finest places to eat, the tastiest dishes to order, and the best sources for gourmet goodies to go, never leaving without something chocolate for dessert. Elizabeth is the consummate hunter-gatherer, buzzing around town with a long to-do list stuffed in her purse, pulling together all the ingredients needed for a drool-worthy dinner for ten. Or twenty. Or fifty.

Yet, somehow (this is a mystery I have yet to solve), she doesn't gain *one* ounce. She will beg to differ, but believe me, I've lunched with Elizabeth for many years and marvel at her ability to enjoy anything from the menu and not wear it on her hips.

Yes, we are still friends.

That third thing? Elizabeth adores books and never leaves home without them. When she sweeps in the door, armed with a classy tote bag overflowing with her latest finds, I know I'll be heading to the nearest bookstore or popping on Amazon soon after she leaves. Her enthusiasm for what she's reading is infectious; the only cure is to buy your own copies ASAP.

Here's what I love most about Elizabeth: Her favorite book is the Bible. In fact, her whole life revolves around the one who wrote it and the timeless wisdom His Word provides. The splendid discussion questions and study guide at the end of this book make her deep faith and strong commitment clear.

When Elizabeth Hoagland says, "Let's be friends," I'd encourage you to say yes, knowing your journey together will be filled with fun and food and, most of all, faith. Her heart's desire is for you to know this vital truth, dear Sister: we have no greater friend than Jesus.

—Liz Curtis Higgs

Introduction

There ain't no surer way to find out whether you like
people or hate them than to travel with them.
—Mark Twain

Welcome, sister-friend. You and I are going to have some kind of fun traveling together. I'll explain shortly.

Quick question: What do you think about when you hear the phrase "road trip"?

Reflecting on my college days, no other delightful duo of words prophesied adventure more than *road trip*. Whether the escapade meant many miles or a few, my friends and I could be ready to go, pronto.

While most of us had classes on Fridays, we simply chose to create a long weekend and be MIA for the day. Our grades dipped as a result, but we hit the road anyway.

Driving through the night was another given, coupled with massive quantities of caffeine. Thankfully, our parents knew none of this.

Our destination wasn't as important as the journey. It was the invaluable gift of time we grabbed to spend with each other, nonstop chatter our real agenda. No stress, only a carefree breeze blowin' through our hair, the Spinners serenading us at high decibels.

A few decades later, I've discovered the exact same excitement of loading up a car still holds true today. Whether with my husband

and children, or with dear friends, the thrill of traveling together woos me in every time.

Sister-friend, you and I are going to take a road trip via this book. Think *Thelma and Louise,* minus the cliff.

I'll be giving you a sneak peek into many uniquely God-orchestrated friendships. You'll get the chance to meet many lovely ladies and see how they changed my life by bringing new opportunities into it. They've been the hinge that opened the door to those opportunities.

While I'd have preferred to kick back on the couch, parked in my comfort zone, you'll see how these persuasive sister-friends lifted me up off that comfy couch, into faith-boosting experiences. Their one little question, "Would you like to_____?" led me to utter a sheepish yes.

I like to call these answers an "uncomfortable yes." You know what I mean? When your first instinct is to say no, but instead, "Yes" falls out of your mouth. Turns out my uncomfortable yeses are some of the best decisions I've ever made. You'll see them sprinkled throughout this book.

Let's take a minute for a little background before we take off. First, I was a hovered-over, micro-managed lonely only. My parents were married for eight years before I came along, and then we were three. Rarely separated.

Though I remained an only child, I didn't stay lonely for long. Over the years, the Lord has blessed me with incredible friends. Some came individually, and some came in groups, which are all blissfully named. (You must know naming things and people is of *monumental* importance to me.)

Second, I'm also blessed with four men and four women in my life: one hubby of over three decades, three sons, three daughters-in-love, and one granddaughter (so far). You may hear a thing or two about them down the road.

As we journey through seasons of friendship together, you'll be blessed by precious pearls of wisdom from some of my friends. They're not only sharing their life's experiences, they've also agreed to share some of their infamous, to-die-for recipes, for which you'll thank me later, trust me. (Fourteen are included in this book, while thirty-two more can be found on my website: www.elizabethhoagland.com.)

Each chapter is a "stop" on our virtual road trip. Each one offers a different shared pursuit for your takeaway: Discovering, Life-Giving, Understanding, Laughing, Soul-Stretching, Mentoring, Praying, Persevering, Shopping, Cheering, and Inviting.

You can bet we will laugh and cry and laugh some more. You'll find antics with my sister-friends worthy of a try with your own friends.

Some of my best and dearest friends arrived in the strangest of circumstances. God knows what He's doing when He delivers a new Jane Doe on your doorstep. Right about the time you're convinced you have the perfect number of friends, our generous Lord will show you otherwise.

Some friends appear daily, some monthly, while others came for only a season. Bottom line? They've *all* taught me something.

There are many ways to look at friendship. Someday, I'd love to be able to approach friendship like Gordy does (he's our middle son). When he was a freshman at the University of Kentucky (UK), I became homesick for him only days after moving him into his dorm. A reunion for lunch promised a quick fix.

I picked Gordy up at an agreed location. After a short distance, we pulled up to a four-way stop. He shouted, "Mom! Honk your horn! There's my friend!"

I quickly honked. This handsome young man was sportin' a vibrant UK blue shirt. When he saw Gordy, he immediately smiled and waved. As Gordy waved back, I asked, "He looks nice, what's his name?"

Gordy replied, "I don't know, but he's my friend."

Oh, that it could be that easy.

C. S. Lewis in his book *The Four Loves* said, "All true friendship begins when one person looks at another and says, 'What? You, too?

I thought I was the only one.'"[1] This, "What? You too?" has become a favorite catchphrase with many of my friends. My prayer is you'll say this to yourself while reading this book, then to your friends, seeing how much we all have in common.

My goal for all of us on this journey is to grow our friendships intentionally and spiritually. Good news: each chapter will offer three sections to help us do this.

First, in "Friendly Encounters," you'll see how the Lord crossed my path with new women, bonding us in a variety of ways depending on the season. The lengths to which He goes are uncanny and comical. Second, "In Their Own Words" is where you'll get to read different treatises (don't miss the word "treat" hidden in that word because you're in for a real treat) from my friends on different topics. Third, in "Inspiration to Go," we'll discuss how this might look in your life and include ideas to try.

The bad news is the journey we're destined to complete is without neither peril nor distractions. It comes with a few curves, hills, and some mountains. We'll encounter various detours. Notice our friendly pronoun, "we." We're *together*, right?

Robert Louis Stevenson said, "We are all travelers in the wilderness of this world, and the best we can find in our travels is an honest friend."

Are you ready? Let's pretend we're hopping in a super svelte convertible (Hey, one can dream), top down, warm sun shinin', of course. First stop is your favorite drive-through. You pick, since you're my guest.

We'll grab some drinks and hit the road while listening to Jamie Grace's song *What a Beautiful Day*. "So put the drop-top down, turn it up, I'm ready to fly!"

Let's go.

First Stop: Discovering
(Friends from Books)

There is no friend as loyal as a book.[1]
—Ernest Hemingway

It's nearly impossible to say no to Lynn Reece.

Back in the day, Lynn was the women's ministry director at Southeast Christian Church in Louisville, Kentucky. She was working wonders in the lives of our women. She orchestrated countless Bible study classes and events for the church, and she organized childcare for young moms. She had an influence on thousands of women of all ages—myself included.

One year, Lynn polled all the Bible study teachers, asking them if women's ministry were to offer something in addition to Bible study, what would it be? The majority of them answered, "A book club."

Lynn called my cousin, Bonnie, and me into her office. Steady as a steamroller, she said, "I want you two to start a book club." Without realizing it, we simultaneously accepted. That was that.

The Lord steered us on a different path, however. The very same week we met with Lynn, Bonnie's father was diagnosed with cancer. Her parents lived out of town, which meant she'd be driving to see them—often. This detour would take her down a very difficult road, causing her to be unable to help lead the book club.

So, there I was—solo! Shakin' in my shoes.

What was originally a relatively easy yes morphed into a very, very, *very* uncomfortable yes. I was the epitome of a female version of Moses when he argued with the Lord in Exodus 6:30 (NLT), "I can't do it! I'm such a clumsy speaker!"

Here was my argument in the form of a pitiful prayer: "No, Lord, not me by myself. I hate to speak in public. I can't speak in public. I don't know how to speak in public. Please send someone else. Thank you very kindly for your *prompt solution* to this matter."

No answer.

Fast-forward a few weeks. Several girls came to my aid. (Looking back now, I realize the Lord did answer by sending these girls. They were angels in disguise.) We set a monthly schedule and prayed over numerous book selections. I remember one time we had forty-five books out on the table, with only nine slots for our season.

Once a month, on a Sunday night, the eve before our Monday-night book club meeting, I'd call Gwen (you'll meet her on our third stop), who was one of the angels in disguise, and say, "This is ridiculous. I'm scared to death. Why are we doing this? Nobody's gonna show up."

To which the Lord howled His head off, I'm certain, because God bless Him—yes, we can bless the Lord—somehow, some way, He held me up and helped me speak. By His mercy and grace, our book club blossomed. It wasn't like anything I'd ever been a part of before.

Friendly Encounters

Besides my family, book club is the best gift God ever gave to me and to those who attended. He brought a handful of women at first (and sometimes men, when we had male authors visit). The handful morphed into many more. Beautiful friendships were forged.

Bibliophiles bonded. We book lovers didn't even need to say, "What? You too?" C. S. Lewis personified our meetings: "You can never get a cup of tea large enough or a book long enough to suit me."[2] That, coupled with "so many books, so little time," was our MO.

We quickly discovered that book club relationships gave women from all walks of life an opportunity to first, get out of the house (oh, yes). And second, it gave them a chance to go deeper. What better way to do that than around a common topic such as a great book? It didn't take long to see ourselves in the characters or drama of a book. When discussion naturally evolved, we were allowing the Lord to work in ways we never would've expected. We found ourselves opening up and letting our guards down.

The book club gals also brought a beautiful bounty of food to each meeting. Food in any equation resulted in more blissful discussion, and before we knew it, our time would be up. This was a good thing, however, causing us to look forward to our next meeting that much more.

Comic relief came early on because of a rather unique book title we selected. It was *The Purse-Driven Life: It Really Is All about Me* by Anita Renfroe. When my new-friend-thanks-to-book-club Linda went into LifeWay to see whether they carried this book, the sales clerk patted her hand and said, "Oh no, honey, you don't mean *The Purse-Driven Life*; you mean *The Purpose-Driven Life*."

The sales clerk genuinely thought Linda was confused, wanting Rick Warren's book. Our selection was a total spoof of Rick's, but in a funny, spiritual way, thanks to Anita's crazy wit. Linda did indeed know what she was talking about.

All of us book clubbers were astonished to discover how many authors we had living nearby. Authors from Kentucky, Indiana, Ohio, and Tennessee were happy to come visit. They graciously entertained our questions, talked about their books, and even signed them for us.

I remember one night getting to interview author Lisa Samson from Lexington. She was a hair on the unpredictable side.

I'd discovered this about her the first time I met her. I drove over to Lexington to take her out for lunch and to become better acquainted with her before she came to our book club.

I was to park at her house, which was close to a restaurant we could walk to. However, the weather did not cooperate. It was raining. Sideways.

Lisa quickly hatched plan B. "Let's make lunch here," she offered. "We can whip up BLTs."

Placing a knife and a cutting board before me, Lisa said, "You slice the tomatoes while I fry the bacon." She plunked down a huge bushel basket full of homegrown tomatoes at my feet. My mouth was watering.

I had to repeatedly whisper to myself, "Just act natural." Sister-friend, I was already a big fan of Lisa's, having read several of her books, my favorite being *Women's Intuition*. Our selection for book club that month was *Straight Up*.

Meanwhile, my attempt at remaining calm was difficult because all I could think of was, *I'm in Lisa Samson's kitchen, and she is frying bacon.*

I learned what a foodie Lisa is that day, homegrown everything sprouting all over her yard. Oh my, it was the best BLT, the best visit, and just the best. (Check out a version of our recipe after our ninth stop.)

About a week later, when we hosted Lisa for our book club meeting, I decided it might be fun for us to perch on stools for the interview. Lisa's way-cool bohemian getup flowed to the floor, a palpable hush filled the room, and everyone sat back in anticipation.

While I was worried about what might transpire, our Q&A flowed beautifully. Lisa's remarks about her writing and passions enlightened all of us, giving us much to consider.

We all savored every second with her. I thought, *Wow, Lord, you are something else to pull this off.*

Jan Watson, another favorite author of mine, also joined us several times. Jan is from Lexington, and she's my hero for many reasons—the top being that she didn't publish her first book until she was sixty years old. She has now written eight books.

She and I became forever friends. Jan is always happy to mentor me and anyone else who falls onto her path. She's divinely generous that way.

One of many threads we have in common is our love for dogs. Terriers, at that. Terribly territorial terriers. When we trade terrier tales, our howling frightens our poor pooches. I digress. God bless Jan.

As time and technology progressed, our book club ventured into the world of Skyping. Authors from far away agreed to Skype with us. What a fun discovery.

Satan was not at all happy about this. He began scrambling our efforts. There was the time when we could see and hear Chris Fabry, but he could only hear us. Then there was the time when we could see Lysa TerKeurst and she could see us, but she couldn't hear us, so we had to talk on our cell phones. I know, pitiful.

Glory be for the time when we had a good connection *both* ways with the one and only Karen Kingsbury. We had close to two hundred ladies that night. My friend Nancy Augiar was there; she's one of three Nancies you'll meet in this book. (To help you keep them straight, I'm naming them; of course I am. This Nancy will heretofore be known as Nancy the Hugging Evangelist—and you'll see why when you officially meet her on our fourth stop.) Anyway, Nancy the Hugging Evangelist got to share a story with Karen about how her book led her to pursue a meaningful career change. Karen began to cry.

One hundred percent of us were in awe of the entire evening. Satan again tried to thwart our efforts, however, by throwing me a curveball. The morning of our meeting, I came down with laryngitis. No voice, not even a squeak. Hot tea couldn't touch it.

I shot an email to my friend Sherry (you'll meet her on our fifth stop) and told her of my dilemma. Without pondering the problem, she said, "I'll run the meeting for you. Send me your notes." Don't forget, this was the day of the meeting. What a brave soul.

Book club met for seven stellar years. During those years, we read close to seventy books. Akin to having to choose one's favorite child, when asked what our favorite book was, I'll tactfully say one of our *many* favorite discoveries is still *Over Salad and Hot Bread: What an Old Friend Taught Me about Life* by Mary Jensen. We loved that little book, which produced a big discussion. Countless book club gals are still talking about it. (A list of our favorites can be found in the back of this book.)

During the years of book club at SEC, I was blessed to meet hundreds of women. To this day, I still call them my book club buddies. We were constantly discovering new authors and ideas. I realize saying yes to book club led to some incredible relationships. Along the way, these wonderful women had a profound impact on my life. I'm convinced our gracious God was at the helm.

In Their Own Words

Bonding over the mutual love of books creates a perfect introduction to a new friend. Like I said, the women I met during my seven-year tenure with the group impacted me far more than I impacted them. And I discovered making friends through a book club started with a common interest: being open; seasons; good distractions; and lingering moments. Let's take a look.

A Common Interest

There are some book club friends I'll never forget. Their ideas and energy have stuck with me. But don't just take my word for it. Take Pat, for example. She makes me smile just to think of her.

Pat's a former children's librarian. She's a voracious reader. We got along famously from the beginning.

One winter morning, with snow covering the ground and blanketing tree branches, Pat invited our mutual friend, Liz, and me over for lunch. She said, "Come casual. We're havin' soup."

Liz and I arrived in snow-boot-casual. Pat greeted us while some sensational aromas wafted through her adorable bungalow. Her kitty cats ran and hid, wondering what possessed us to invade their home.

God bless Pat. Y'all, she made not one, not two, but *three* pots of soup. We had quite the soup-a-thon. (You're being awarded one of the recipes at the end of this stop.) That special day, Pat sent us home with containers full of the other soups. Our families had never been so happy.

Pat talks about friendship coming from books. Not only do books keep her company, but friends who love books, she discovered, are what make her life rich. I agree with her. Let's see what this looks like from Pat:

Books have been my friends as long as I can remember. As I sat on the front porch of my grandparents' house reading, I was swept away on many adventures and made countless imaginary friends.

As I walked through the door of the public library in my small hometown when I was a little girl, the wondrous smell of books overwhelmed me... as it still does today... public library, school library, college library, church library, bookstores... ah... that wondrous smell!

I took a job in an elementary school library just to get my foot in the door of the library world. God opened that door for me and gently nudged me in, and I never left. I was immersed in the aroma of books (and kids) once more! Now, I miss that smell and those precious children... many who have become adult friends.

Those friendships touch my heart even today. Sometimes we hosted authors in that library. More friendships formed because of the stories within those books. I was in awe of their creativity with connecting words to tell a story. I'm not a writer. I'm an organizer, but I'm also a reader who consumes books, hungry for more. Those authors' love for writing and my love for reading forged our friendships.

God then opened another door and brought me to the book club. That opened a whole new world... a whole new group of books, authors, and friends... all connected to Him.

My faith is the most important part of my life, but there is another constant that has remained.

I've always needed books.

I've always needed friends.

And I've always needed friends who need books.

I just love how Pat used books to make connections with people. She carried that spirit into our book club.

Being Open

Diane is another gal I met via the book club. We've become dear friends, not only from the club, but because of our children, plus we're in Bible study together. Diane likes to say, "Fifty is the new thirty," at least that's what she said at our milestone birthday parties.

She talks about how book clubs and friendships can happen in unexpected ways. They don't have to be official or formal, if you're open to whatever opportunity comes along:

> Whether you're still raising teenagers, or soon to be a grandma, it's a blessing to be surrounded by friends sharing the journey. Hebrews 10:24 says, "And let us consider how we may spur one another on toward love and good deeds" (NLT).
>
> Another bonus of passing five decades is now my schedule permits reading some of those books I love but didn't have time to enjoy when I was driving carpool, attending field hockey matches, or making family dinners. After all, I was an English major in college, so the desire to read is practically part of my DNA.
>
> Book clubs don't have to be formal meetings. My dad and I swap books almost every time we get together. Both of my parents love to read and in the process, it gives us new topics to discuss when we get together. We purposefully choose books that are meaningful and thought provoking, not just the latest summer beach read.

> At Christmas time, I always give my daughter and two daughters-in-law the same book so we can all read it together. Sometimes my selection is a big hit and sometimes it's a flop! This is a fun way I can learn about what interests them and they can know what interests me as well.
>
> So whether you like the current best seller, or the classics, keep reading. You might just make some great friends in the process!

Diane nails the concept of being open. She and I have met countless gals of all ages who we'd have never met had it not been for our book clubs.

You'll never believe it, but some of these gals arrived in the form of guardian angels. I am finally realizing I've had, and *still* have, many guardian angels. These gals don't think they're anything out of the ordinary, but the Lord has shown me they are.

Seasons

The first guardian angel I discovered was a beautiful and wise woman named Margaret Julian. We all called her "Miss Margaret." I'm awarding her this guardian angel title posthumously, as she's been in heaven for a few years now.

She came to babysit for us when Woody was a baby. Those were holy days when Miss Margaret entered the front door.

I met Miss Margaret before book club was a glimmer in God's eye; however, she had her very own, private book club, which planted seeds in me for when the time came. Margaret was a one-book type of girl. You can guess she only read from the Good Book, God's Word, many times sharing what she was learning. I believe she was heaven-sent to our little family, à la Mary Poppins.

Miss Margaret made each of us feel special and hummed hymns

as she went about her day. Mostly she babysat, graciously saving my sanity, but occasionally she'd throw in a load of laundry or whip up some spaghetti. The only thing she was adamant about *not* doing was ironing. We were on the same page there.

One afternoon, however, I came home while the boys were napping. The basement door was ajar, and I smelled something out of the ordinary. I dashed down the steps. Not meaning to, seems I scared the wits out of Miss Margaret. She jumped a mile in the air while hollering, "Oh, sweet Jesus! You've caught me!"

There she was, ironing *sheets* for the guestroom bed, as my parents were coming to stay for the weekend. She wanted them to be ultra comfy, God bless her.

Some Wednesdays, Miss Margaret would arrive before John left for work. She loved his coffee (as all of my friends do). When he offered her a cup, she said, "No, John, not today. I'm fasting."

John wouldn't hear of it. "Come on, Miss Margaret, I've even got some good ol' whippin' cream to go in it."

With that, she said in a very loud voice, "Go on, John. Get behind me, Satan!" Wide-eyed, we busted out laughing. John never again interfered with her fasting.

As Margaret aged and her health deteriorated, culminating in a stroke, the boys and I would visit her periodically (not as often as we'd have liked). Yet her legacy of caregiving lives on as her daughter, Brenda, and her granddaughter Dazsarae helped take care of my mother when she was in a nursing home. Brenda and I still stay in touch and call each other sisters.

Good Distractions

Another guardian angel arrived when our boys were in middle and high school at Christian Academy of Louisville. Her name is Luly (90 percent of Louisvillians know Luly). Luly's daughter, Libby, was in John Jr.'s class, and Luly was the PTO president, so 100 percent of Christian Academy parents knew her.

One night, John and I dropped our boys off at a home football game and went to a dinner party nearby. (No comment from the peanut gallery.) Halfway into the dinner, we got a phone call. It was Luly. She informed us that Gordy had been hurt.

Never mind he and his friends weren't playing football on the field; they were running and chasing each other underneath the bleachers. That was where Gordy crashed head-on into one of the steel poles. I know.

John's brother Billy, who's a doctor, just happened to be at the football game. Thank you, Lord. Luly found him, and Billy kept Gordy calm, in spite of the fact nobody knew who he was at first because there was so much blood on his face. (Thankful I didn't witness that, or they'd have been reviving me too.) Luly was our guardian angel that night.

Even though our kids are now married and have children, Luly and I still manage to grab lunch or get our hubbies and meet up for dinner. Over lunch one day, Luly reminded me we'd both lived through illnesses and subsequent deaths of both of our parents.

We surprised each other when we were able to quote different Medicare regulations to each other, cracking up because this was an education we had *zero* desire to acquire. The blessing was, we supported each other during those difficult days. Another big "What? You too?"

Because Libby is an only child, once Luly and Greg took her to college, I knew a distraction or two (or ten) was in order. Enter book club. Luly quickly began attending and recounts her experience:

> I discovered this was a wonderful, diverse group of women in different stages of life who gathered monthly. Some may not have even read that month's selection, but they all had something to share. Some women needed insight, others would offer some, then there were those of us who could simply sit and relax, taking it all in.

One month, the book club featured an out of town author, Erin Smalley. Her book we discussed was *Grown-Up Girlfriends: Finding Real Friends in the Real World* by Erin and her friend, Carrie Oliver. It was hugely eye-opening to me in the way she discussed the different baskets of friendships we can experience in a lifetime as we change. Erin fielded loads of questions, walking us through her excellent suggestions.

This was just what I needed. I was dealing with some guilt over friendships that had changed as my daughter had grown and I wasn't in the day-to-day with the moms of her friends we'd spent so many years together, while raising our kids. That was in my late forties.

Now in my late fifties, I have a better appreciation for the value of long lasting friendships. Even the value of those I had, but have moved on from, still helped make me a better friend today.

Whether nurturing your friendship happens thanks to a book club, or a simple lunch out, don't miss out on why the Lord has brought that person into your life.

I love how Luly captures the truth that changing seasons are embraceable. She also learned to appreciate them and move on. (This is a lesson I've needed more than once.)

Lingering Moments

Several years ago, our book clubbers from SEC were looking for a place to hold a summer Bible study. Enter yet one more guardian angel named Nancy Tinnell. (She'll be heretofore known as Guardian Angel Nancy.) She was the first to jump on this opportunity for a

Bible study, allowing us to meet at her church, Middletown United Methodist.

She added to the plot by suggesting Jane Chilton (you'll meet her on our third stop) and I team-teach with her. This was a major uncomfortable yes, as I'd never really taught a large Bible study before. Good news was, these two seasoned teachers were taking me under their wings, and we'd be taking turns.

This was the year we read Liz Curtis Higgs's book on Ruth, *The Girl's Still Got It: Take a Walk with Ruth and the God Who Rocked Her World.* We had a blast teaching a night-time class and a morning one. It was one of the most rewarding experiences I've had. As an added bonus, Lizzie was the bomb and made a guest appearance at one of our classes.

Guardian Angel Nancy's a little like Jane in that she pushes you out of your comfort zone, fully confident you're capable when you know you yourself are *not*. This is where God gets to show off, which is way cool to watch.

Guardian Angel Nancy often uses a phrase that melts my heart. Her prayers often thank the Lord for His "canopy of grace." You feel like you can crawl right up into His lap and hide for a while.

She recently shared another fabulous phrase: "lingering moments." Listen to her explanation:

> Lingering moments. That's what I call them. Lunch with friends is about to wrap up, and I desperately want to linger over just one more glass of iced tea before going back to my office, or, depending on the day of the week, heading home to laundry and various other won't-go-away chores.
>
> My friends and I cover a lot of territory in our lunch escapes, catching up on news of children and grandchildren, rehashing our Tuesday morning Bible

study discussions, or talking about books, movies, and travel. When we venture into entertainment or movie discussions, I might be inclined to mention Tom Selleck too frequently, but my friends are always there to put me back on track! Sometimes our conversation is so enjoyable I don't want to give it up. I need those lingering moments with my friends.

On rare occasions, the lingering moment evolves into a week-long girlfriend getaway. We pack our books, sunscreen, and swimsuits (promising we will *not* take pictures of one another by the pool) and head south to the beach, kissing our understanding husbands goodbye.

Escapes to the beach are not a frequent indulgence for most people, and sometimes it's just as difficult for me to schedule a luncheon lingering moment. Through my books, however, I am able to have small escapes on a daily basis.

I run away for a bit by picking up a book from my nightstand and allowing it to introduce me to places, characters, and time periods that can teach and inspire, make me laugh, cry, or be filled with a sense of wonder.

Reading may be a solitary activity, but discussing your impressions of a book in a book club with others adds an important dimension to the learning experience. When you escape into the same book that others are reading, it's great fun to share opinions and ideas. Some of our book club members have had significant spiritual experiences through our books. As much as a good book may bless, I feel an even greater blessing because of the new friends I've made. They share their hearts and their wisdom each month.

Don't you just love the idea of lingering moments? They capture what my heart (and I suspect yours too) longs for in friendship. More. More time with a trusted friend. More utterances of "What? You too?" More laughter.

You're getting this, right? How gracious of our God. He is the one who led us to discover sweet lingering moments from saying yes to the book club all those years ago.

Inspiration to Go

Whether you're in a book club or looking to start one, the spiritual benefit can be invaluable. Not only do you grow closer to each other, you grow closer to God.

Maybe your book club is with friends from all over the country, and you talk via Skype: a veritable *world* of opportunities to discover.

Or maybe your book club hires a teenage babysitter so you can connect with young moms. (This idea came from my new friend and wise-beyond-her-years editor, Becky Nesbitt. Where was this idea when my boys were little? Y'all *run* with this.)

Maybe you invite your neighbors over for coffee and ask them to bring their favorite book. This could birth a book club in your neighborhood.

Maybe your book club is on email only. Yes, you can email questions out to your virtual club, and they can respond to the group on their own time.

Elizabeth Barrett Browning said, "No man can be called friendless who has God and the companionship of good books." As you can tell, sister-friend, attending a book club is a beneficial activity for all ages. It's an opportunity to expand your reading horizon as well as your faith while you make new friends, as you discover many new things. (Don't forget to check out book recommendations at the end of this book.)

Next stop? I can hardly wait for you to meet my Ya-Ya Sisters. Hot tip: grab a handful of Kleenex before you rejoin us

Not-Too-Spicy Taco Soup
(from Pat Hall)

This is one of the three soups Pat served Liz and me on that cold, winter day I told you about. This soup was our favorite and has become our kids' as well as our friends' favorite. I usually double the recipe so we have leftovers or have some to take to someone in need of a meal.

Other than frying the hamburger, you basically open the cans of the ingredients below and throw them in. No rocket science here. I make mine in a crock-pot so it can simmer all day. Great for football game watchin' or tailgatin'.

Ingredients

1 pound of hamburger
½ chopped onion (I omit this, not being a fan of onions, but you decide.)
1 can white corn
1 can ranch beans
1 can Rotel tomatoes
1 can diced tomatoes
1 can pinto beans (I substitute black beans only because I'm not endeared to pinto beans and because the black beans make the soup more Mexican-ish. All educated chefs just rolled their eyes over that little comment.)
1 can diced green chilies
1 package taco seasoning
1 package ranch dressing

Directions

- Brown the hamburger, draining off the grease. Add the taco seasoning with the required amount of water, stirring until thickened. Set aside so that if you're using the onion, you can brown it in a separate pan with a little bit of olive oil. Once the onion is browned, you can add all the cans, the meat, and the ranch mix, allowing it all to simmer.

- Either a big soup pot on the stove or a crock-pot works well.
- Pat has tried this with Italian sausage instead of hamburger and said it's good that way too. We both like serving this with a little bit of sour cream, shredded cheddar cheese, and corn bread, Fritos, or tortilla chips. Enjoy.

Second Stop: Life-Giving (Friends Thanks to Our Kids: The Ya-Yas)

Friends matter. They are the butter that makes our grits
so savory and the pepper that gives them a kick.[1]
—Deborah Ford

Orientation day at a new school always made my stomach flip. Please tell me why, as a parent, the same scenario would surface?

This particular orientation day was for our oldest son, John Jr., who was entering first grade at our neighborhood school. We arrived with time to spare, for a change. However, that spare time disappeared like a mist because of getting the stroller out, putting Woody in it, and getting Gordy out of his car seat.

Neither of the younger two boys were especially in good moods, thence the bag of Cheerios, juice boxes, and several other bribes up my sleeve. The extra-large diaper bag that seemed like such a good idea at the time was now tipping in around seventy-five pounds. Feigning excitement for John Jr., off we went.

Thankfully, many volunteer tour guides awaited us bewildered moms, motioning where to go. The tour guide we were matched up with walked right up to us. She made direct eye contact with John Jr., declaring with great enthusiasm, "Welcome to Dunn Elementary School. What grade will you be in?"

Already considering this cute gal courageous to grab our challenging group of four newbies, I relaxed. She whisked us down the halls, showing John Jr. where his classroom was and where the lunchroom was (thankfully, no nauseating aromas were emanating from it that day), and gave us hefty paperwork disguised as a welcome packet.

Our guide's name was Kathy. She and I talked nonstop out of the starting gate. Early into our tour, Kathy suggested we meet for lunch one day. Figuring I could use a friend at this new school, I accepted.

A couple of weeks later, Kathy and I met at a quaint bistro. She proceeded to tell me she and her husband, Joe, had recently moved to Louisville. They had a daughter who'd also be in first grade and a son who'd be in second.

After we chatted for a while, she said, "You know, I've been praying the Lord would lead me to a Christian friend. I think you're the one."

Sister-friend, I *acted* like I was her answer. I didn't even consider myself a Christian then. Her words were like positive prophecy spoken right over me.

I had joined a Bible study a few years prior to this, but the truth is I still wasn't getting it yet. Homework stayed up in my head, far, far, far away from my heart. I fully believe the Lord sent Kathy to lead me to more friends and to a closer relationship with Him. God's timing never ceases to amaze me.

Kathy became what I like to call a life-giving friend. You know, the type of friend who adds something to your life every time you see them. They become crucial to your life, and you don't know what you'd do without them. And they constantly point you to Christ.

Friendly Encounters

While they may start out accidently or over some casual event, like new school orientation, life-giving friendships don't just happen. They are the result of showing up and being available, time and time again. Kathy showed me what this looks like.

After that fateful lunch meeting, Kathy and I were forever bonded. And all thanks to our children becoming friends, we met five other families who also became very close friends. We were (and are) quite the coterie, experiencing, "What? You too?" at every gathering.

Kathy is the one who came up with our moniker, "The Ya-Yas." Kathy found a gold plaque she bought for all of us to hang in our homes. It reads: "Ya-Yas: A group of three or more women whose hearts and souls are joined together by laughter and tears shared throughout the glorious journey of life."

The elementary years flew by, and suddenly, fifth grade graduation was upon us. During the rehearsal, Kathy and I were decorating the gym while the kids were practicing their song. We wept buckets of tears for two reasons: One was the astonishing fact our first graders were now fifth graders, bound for middle school.

The second and saddest reason was Kathy and Joe and their kids would soon be moving to Cincinnati. Joe had been hired as a football coach at the University of Cincinnati. This was good news for him to return to coaching.

His only noncoaching job had been the one he'd had in Louisville. He told us many years later that that job was his least favorite job he ever had. The Romans 8:28 version of that, I'm thrilled to report, produced lifelong friends we'd never have had, had Joe not taken that job. ("And we know that in *all* things God works for the good of those who love him, who have been called according to his purpose.")

Kathy and Joe moved to Cincinnati that summer. Once football season kicked into gear, several of us went to visit and cheer Joe's team on, on several occasions. Five families lived in Louisville while Kathy and Joe began their new lives in Cinci.

It wasn't long until Jim Tressel became the new head coach of the Ohio State Buckeyes. "Tress," as they call him, called Joe with an invitation for him to coach the quarterbacks at Ohio State. This was a fantastic opportunity for Joe. But another move, and further away this time.

We quickly studied up on the team's colors (and shopped accordingly), their mascot, their marching band (infamously known as TBDBITL—shouldn't spell it out for young eyes), and their season's schedule. Sometimes together, and sometimes separately, our five families trekked to Columbus to cheer, "Go Bucks!" a thousand and one times.

Kathy and Joe's paradise became complete when their son, Matthew (thenceforth known as Matt D.), made the football team while their daughter, Kaitlin, made the cheerleading squad. Seeing the three of them on the field while Kathy cheered from the stands took our breath away. (Joe usually headed up to the press box in the sky.)

One year, Joe's brilliant coaching earned one of his quarterbacks, Troy Smith, the Heisman Trophy. This was huge. We all watched the long-anticipated awards program on TV together. As we scanned the crowd for Kathy and Joe, suddenly, Troy's name was called. Our guys were ecstatic, while the girls kept looking for Kathy and Joe. We finally saw the backs of their heads. We waved, pretending they could see us (I know).

Kathy later showed us pictures from the entire evening. All we could talk about were the fabulous shoes she wore: high heels any female would salivate over, worthy of being in a museum with a brass plaque: "These to-die-for heels were worn at a Heisman Trophy Award Night." Our guys were incredulous. Go figure.

Joe's Italian heritage brought out the best in Kathy. After the games, she cooked up some of the finest, most mouthwatering Italian meals I've ever tasted. She also cooked for Joe's quarterbacks many a night. No worries, permission was granted, making even the meatballs compliant. (Don't miss the secret recipe from her and Matt D. at the end of the sixth stop.)

One rainy night, however, paradise became postponed, after one phone call. This was our first Ya-Ya detour. Kathy called all of us to report Joe had had a heart attack.

"It gets worse," she said, her voice barely audible. "They've found a spot on his kidney. It's cancer. They've given him six months to live."

Tears still fall as I relive this moment. Our small, safe, and secure group had never encountered the "C" word before, nor did we know what to do with it. This detour was one big uncomfortable yes we would tackle, coupled with one education none of us signed up for. We were in knee-deep now, and we were determined to fight for Joe, right there on our knees. We were reminded of Proverbs 12:25: "Anxiety weighs down the heart, but a kind word cheers it up."

But that's what life-giving friends do. They not only live life together when things are good, they are there for you when life gets tough. And just when you think you're failing, or are at a loss for words, not sure of your next step, they teach you. In the little things.

Because of Joe's incredible determination, plus the power of thousands of prayer warriors' prayers, coupled with a most gracious God, Joe lived five and a half more years. I'd still like to have a word with the doctor who originally said he only had six months to live, but I might not be very lady-like. Honestly, I believe it was God's way of showing us His timing is better than what we think or believe while here on earth.

This was straight out of Ephesians 3:20–21: "Now to him who is able to do immeasurably more than all we ask or imagine, according to his power that is at work within us, to him be glory in the church and in Christ Jesus through all generations for ever and ever! Amen."

During Joe's illness, Kathy kept us informed of his prayer needs. She accepted this new season with grace, diving in headfirst. She was Joe's advocate, and nothing, and I mean *nothing*, was getting by her without strict investigation. She taught us he was living with, not dying of, cancer.

During this time, I fell in love with a sign that says, "Fear not tomorrow ... God is already there." The sign hangs in each of our kitchens, but when Joe was hospitalized on several occasions, Kathy toted that sign with her to hang in his hospital room.

Was Kathy tearful and fearful? Yes, at times, which allowed us to cry along with her, praying even harder. Ever stalwart, she clung to her faith and kept a positive attitude like her life depended on it. She lived out James 1:2–4: "Consider it pure joy, my brothers and sisters, whenever you face trials of many kinds, because you know that the testing of your faith produces perseverance. Let perseverance finish its work so that you may be mature and complete, not lacking anything."

But we cannot forget the silver lining to all of this: Kathy and Joe's first grandchild did get to meet Joe and be held by Joe; he was named after Joe and was photographed multiple times with Joe. All their grandkids affectionately address their grandfather in heaven as Papa Joe. We praise you, Lord.

In Their Own Words

My life-giving friends are truly that—life giving. They are dearer to me than I can explain. It's often not what they say, it's what they do, day in and day out, that makes all the difference in my life. I found my life-giving friends have some amazing qualities. They show up, play together, and create traditions with major intentionality.

Showing Up

Our families that make up the Ya-Yas did so much together, they became life-giving friends over the years because they kept showing up, time and time again. Kathy describes us for you:

> These relationships grew because we had two things in common: our children and a burning desire to grow our relationship with the Lord through Bible studies, prayer, and fellowship.
>
> We showed up for PTA, read stories on library day, and ran with our children in turkey trots. We counted heads on field trips and applauded at piano recitals. Youth sports, Cub Scouts, backyard camp outs, and a host of other kiddo commitments filled our calendars. We shared drinks of choice from tea to Diet Dr. Pepper, a wine here and there, Friday night fare, and church activities. What solidified these unbreakable bonds, setting into motion the countless memories, were our children.
>
> We promised each other confidentiality, prayers, non-judgmental support, and trust for our secrets kept safe. Don't even try asking. The unspoken Ya-Ya Creed: unconditional love and acceptance.
>
> We don't give up or quit; we pray, email, text, call, and nudge each other along the path. Sometimes baby steps are all we can muster, but we take steps hand in hand, heart to heart.
>
> My daughter Kaitlin noticed that her aunt Ya-Yas were generous, respectful, honest, and forgiving of each other. She said, "No matter what, you show up for each other." She then repeated what her dad told her through

> the years: "If you can count your friends on one hand, you are richly blessed." She wrapped up her comments with something like, "Momma, you are really rich."
>
> As of this writing, it's 2017, the year of the Ya-Ya silver anniversary. I sit thoughtfully, watching my daughter snuggle with her baby daughter. I pray the lessons in love and friendship she took from the Ya-Yas will be shared for many generations to come. Five Ya-Yas on one hand. I am richly blessed.

Arm in arm, my life-giving friends are still learning to live out Romans 5:3–4: "We can rejoice, too, when we run into problems and trials, for we know that they help us develop endurance. And endurance develops strength of character, and character strengthens our confident hope of salvation" (NLT).

I love this verse because it shows us we will become stronger Christians as we press on toward eternity. These trials toughen us up for what's ahead. God goes before you and me, giving us a team of sister-friends to hold us up (see Isaiah 52:12, Deuteronomy 31:8, and Psalm 139:5).

We Ya-Yas love our name, but we realized we had the added challenge of what to call our husbands. When Matt D. and Jenny married on a hot summer evening in northern Ohio, the Ya-Yas and our husbands hung out right in front of a large, industrial fan, trying to stay cool.

Jenny's family's farm is in the middle of Amish country. The reception was under a huge tent on the farm where we could watch horse-driven buggies roll down the road. Quite the backdrop.

One of the guys remarked, "Well, if you girls are the Ya-Yas, what are we?"

Steve said, "Yo-Yos—'cuz we're a bunch of yo-yos."

Sadly, for the guys, their name stuck.

Further funny, now that several of the Yas-n-Yos are becoming grandparents, these babies are declared "Ya-Yos-in-Training." (Between the six of us, we're blessed with twelve grandchildren and several more on the way. Is God beyond gracious, or what?)

Joe was able to attend Matt and Jenny's wedding. He looked great. We declared him a miracle. Maybe in denial, we kept doing life. Joe kept on coaching, and we didn't discuss the possibility of a funeral. When you don't talk about it, it won't happen, right?

Joe went to be with Jesus on December 4, 2011. Decisions had to be made. The Louisville Ya-Yas waited. Kathy and her children quickly planned Joe's funeral. She called the Ya-Yas and asked if we'd be "flower bearers." None of us were familiar with this phrase, but of course we answered yes.

At the funeral, following the casket and its pallbearers, the five of us held large baskets overflowing with beautiful, sweet-smelling flower arrangements. The Ya-Ya procession marched slowly down the aisle, placing the arrangements on the altar, fighting back fresh tears.

When the funeral was over, we exited the chapel, and TBDBITL played. There wasn't a tearless face anywhere. Witnessing a sea of massive football players weeping polished me and everyone else off.

Kathy never wavered in her faith. Her constant time spent in God's Word empowered her to just do the next thing, attending to the many guests. While the funeral was a celebration of Joe's life, the reception afterwards, complete with snow falling outside, was also celebratory and incredibly joyful.

If I had to come up with a phrase to attach to Kathy, it would be "spiritual doctor." She not only encourages each of us to maintain our physical health, she's been the prescription we've needed to maintain our spiritual health. (This is a bonus aspect of life-giving friends.)

Playing Together

While Joe's funeral is a bittersweet memory among the Yas-n-Yos, one of our all-time favorite cheerful memories together rings fresh with melt-in-your-mouth s'mores. That's because our crew of life-giving friends does know how to hang out and play. What we tried one night is something you and your family and friends can do together. But be warned: getting your beauty rest is not part of this program.

While I wasn't a big fan of Joan Rivers, she and I did share a distaste for camping.

Joan said, "My idea of camping is staying in a hotel room that only has a plain bathtub and not a Jacuzzi." Amen, Joan, let's rough it together.

My better half loves to camp. He took our boys camping numerous times, but I usually managed to find an excuse not to go. Not wanting me to miss out, John decided a neighborhood campout, where we invited a few friends and neighbors to camp in our own backyard, would be an appealing idea.

I confess if one has to camp, having one's bathroom a short jaunt up the hill is ingenious. The other key contributing factor to entice the children to join in the fun is to guarantee the creation of s'mores as well as the building of a gigantic bonfire. (Aren't all children pyromaniacs?) C. S. Lewis said, "Is any pleasure on earth as great as a circle of Christian friends by a good fire?"[2]

Our fondest memories are from the first year we hosted this great campout. All the Yas-n-Yos plus some neighbors came with children, tents, and mountainous piles of food in tow.

Early into the setup, it became painfully obvious some were more experienced campers than others. Take John Combs, for example. He's been a Boy Scout leader for years. (His and Jayne's son, Drew, later became an Eagle Scout.) Their tent had more than one room and a front porch. Huh?

While the Combses were light-years ahead of all of us, Kathy and Joe could've used a wee bit more equipment, perhaps. While they arrived seemingly ready with their tent and cooler in hand, challenge was they had a two-man tent for their family of four.

For dinner, the guys grilled hamburgers and hot dogs. We all made ooey-gooey s'mores around the bonfire, delighting both adults and children. Our kids had a complete blast, which made the whole night that much more fun for the adults.

The highlight of the night came when my John busted out the boom box. We'd just returned from a trip to Cancun, Mexico, where we'd learned a new dance. We knew our neighbors and the Yas-n-Yos would love to learn this dance.

Turns out the children wanted to learn as much as the parents did. We were a sight to behold in our backyard woods, under the stars that night. The dance? Ah, sister-friend, the Macarena, of course.

I still don't know how we got everyone to turn in, stuffing themselves into their sleeping bags. (I'm wondering now why I didn't sneak back up the hill and jump into our own bed.) I can still hear Kathy, Joe, Kaitlin, and Matt D. howling from being crammed into that tiny two-man tent.

Ever the optimist, Kathy kept saying, "Oh, we'll make it work."

Sleep finally befell us until about three o'clock in the morning. That's when little Megan said, "What's that animal outside our tent, Daddy, and why is it making that noise?"

John reminded me it was a coyote, of all things, having the audacity to howl near our camp. Thankfully, it didn't try to enter any of our tents. Somehow, we all fell back asleep, never realizing those memories would bond our friendships forever.

Traditions while Being Intentional

Looking back now, I realize there was a method to our madness. A new practice amongst the Ya-Yas came about not too long ago. The Ya-Yas are blessed with a calendar girl, otherwise known as Jayne. Nobody keeps us more organized than she does. Whenever we get together, Jayne will always shoot us an email, saying, "Bring your calendars."

Other times, she'll email, saying, "Random dinner." Then she'll throw us dates to meet up for a quick bite one night, and majority rules. These are easy, simple ways to coordinate your friends. Jayne is a vision of 1 Corinthians 14:40: "But all things should be done decently and in order" (ESV). She's a retired schoolteacher. Need I say more?

Sophie Hudson must have friends like the Ya-Yas because she says, "Life is infinitely richer when people are our priority."[3] If these life-giving friends taught me nothing else, they taught me to make the most of every moment. Some moments were more special because of traditions.

It was Jayne who came up with the idea of the Ya-Ya handkerchief. She found a store in town that specializes in monogramming. She found a beautiful handkerchief, trimmed in lace, and had it monogrammed with "Ya-Ya" on it.

Its purpose is to be held in the palm of our hand when we march down the aisle at our children's weddings. Perfect for those tears we're sure to shed. Comfort can be felt from the other five Ya-Yas, enabling the current mother of the groom or mother of the bride to actually make it down the aisle.

When I asked Jayne to explain this little keepsake, she said of the Ya-Yas:

> Life-giving refers to sustaining one another. Compromise is an integral part of sustaining. We Ya-Yas reached a compromise with the now infamous Ya-Ya handkerchief.
>
> The initial idea was to unify us at wedding receptions… perhaps a group serenade to the bride and groom, recite an original poem, or choreograph a sequence of dance steps. Through the brainstorming process, it quickly became evident several of us suffer from stage fright or performance anxiety. (Cue the violins.) We found the compromise we were searching for in our shared, monogrammed handkerchief.

> As we approach our golden years and reflect on our twenty-five-year friendships, we consider long-range plans to live in the same senior facility. (You think I'm kidding? I'm not.) That is exactly what life-giving friendships do. They sustain and support us to the end of life's journey. Tucked away in one of our treasure boxes will be that little white handkerchief, continuing to be a thread in the tapestry that unified us and kept us connected over the years.

We've been passing the handkerchief back and forth to each other as numerous weddings have transpired. Thus far, ten out of the thirteen Ya-Yo children are married. This is a fab gift you and your friends may wish to pass back and forth when you hit the wedding season.

Our handkerchief deserved frequent-flyer miles the year two of our boys married three months apart, in between Susan's two children marrying six weeks apart. How we all showed up at the right wedding, at the right time, in the right city, is still a mystery.

Susan's our theme queen. You can imagine with all these weddings, the Ya-Yas have hosted every type of shower imaginable. Susan runs with any theme to lengths none of us would've ever conjured up. (You'll see her in action on our next stop.)

Denise is a God-send as well. Her job at Etcetera, a local gift and stationery shop, bailed us out of thousands of decisions resulting in over-the-top exquisite invitations for all those showers. No wonder she entertains so effortlessly. (Don't miss her salmon recipe at the end of the eighth stop.)

Bev is the sixth of the Ya-Yas. She is the most proficient multitasker I've ever met. She also cooks up some fine food for the Yas-n-Yos on many occasions. (Don't miss her sausage appetizer.)

The Yas-n-Yos now have another detour. Summer of 2016

presented us with something we weren't familiar with: Bev's husband, Steve, was diagnosed with Parkinson's. While some of our family members are living with this disease, this still sucker-punched us.

We've made a pact to support them whenever and however we can. We've taken on this challenge together. It's another uncomfortable yes, but we're all in. Steve looks great and is in good spirits. His positive attitude will certainly be to his advantage. We're collectively praying as we learned to pray for Joe.

I believe our Yas-n-Yos are unique because not only are the wives good friends, the husbands also get along swimmingly. Some of our Yo-Yos have retired, so they're finding new things to do together. Our children also get along beautifully. Some as you know are having babies, who we pray will also become friends.

First Corinthians 13:7 reminds me of these dear life-giving sister-friends: "Love never gives up, never loses faith, is always hopeful, and endures through *every circumstance*" (NLT, emphasis mine). No matter the occasion or detour, we endure together.

Inspiration to Go

Do you have life-giving friends in your life? Don't overlook the ones already there. Take it from Kathy: a life-giving friend doesn't have to be a perfect friend:

> We complain about chores and prefer reservations to cooking. We whine over unwanted rolls and wrinkles and share the latest in fountain-of-youth remedies. I dare to mention the six-week silver root touch-ups that are scheduled a year in advance. A Ya-Ya will never miss her root touch-up. Okay … truth is … there's one exception … if the grand darlin' is born on the day of services, she will reschedule.

Sister-friend, start small. Maybe it's a plaque you give your friends or a random dinner. Maybe it's a campout in the backyard (or a hotel, maybe). Maybe something monogrammed, like our handkerchief. Whatever it is, make your friendships life-giving.

Picture one of those classic weighing scales (not the kind you step on; they should be burned). When I'm down about something, one or more of the Ya-Yas comes over or calls and brings me back into balance. We've even had to call a couple of emergency meetings, but the blessing comes from just being together.

The next group of gals you'll meet is one I never thought I'd be a part of. Me, go to a Bible study? Not a chance. Until…

Hearty Fight-over-It Sausage Appetizer
Warning: Men beg for this after they've had it the first time.
(from Bev Fleece)

Our dear Bev brought this appetizer to one of our Ya-Yo gatherings many years ago. Upon trying it, the Yo-Yos never left their positions and parked around the table where it was being served. This made it challenging for us Ya-Yas to partake, not to mention the scowls on our husbands' faces, as if they had no intention of sharing with us.

Shockingly, our children now behave the same way. While this dish is delicious for men and women, its heartiness is what appeals to our boys.

Initially, Bev made it by rolling up the sausage mixture into portions of crescent rolls. Once baked, she'd slice the rolls as you would a loaf of bread, and we'd eat them that way. It was a little labor-intensive, until my friend Anne Arnold investigated the below recipe. (She was so enamored with this appetizer after I brought it to her dinner party when our friends, the Daltons, visited. Anne immediately dove in, researching different variations.) Thanks to Anne and our good buddy, the Pillsbury Doughboy, he's taught us a much easier method.

This variation includes an additional variety of cheese, because for sure we all *need* more cheese.

Ingredients
Appetizer
2 cans crescent rolls

2 pounds of spicy pork sausage (Here in Louisville, Kentucky, we're blessed with Purnell's sausage, but Bob Evans or any variety will do if you can't find Purnell's. Plus, if you don't want it on the hot side, just use mild or medium sausage.)

2 packages of cream cheese

2 cups of shredded sharp cheddar cheese

Sauce

Equal parts of:

Dijon mustard

Apricot preserves

Honey

For this sized appetizer, try ⅓ of a cup of each of the ingredients for the sauce. Stir and serve at room temperature with the sausage squares. The sauce is what makes the dish.

Directions

- Preheat oven to 375 degrees.
- In a large skillet, brown the sausage, crumbling it up into small pieces, over medium heat, stirring frequently, until no longer pink. Drain the grease and remove the sausage from the skillet. Add the cream cheese to the same skillet, cooking over low heat until melted. Add the sausage back in, stirring to coat.
- Unroll one can of crescent roll dough into two long rectangles onto the bottom of an ungreased 13 × 9 (three-quart) glass baking dish, pressing over the bottom of the pan and about ½ inch up the sides to form the crust. Spoon sausage and cream cheese mixture evenly over the crust in the baking dish. Sprinkle with the shredded cheddar cheese.
- Unroll second can of crescent rolls and press to form the rectangle, covering the sausage and cheese. Press perforations to seal. (You can also use the crescent sheets, which are now available in some groceries that are all one piece, if you don't want to fool with the perforations of the crescent rolls.)
- Bake for 20–25 minutes, 'til the crescent dough is nicely browned.
- Cool for 10–15 minutes.
- Cut into squares and serve with the sauce. (Watch it disappear.)
- New discovery: If there are any leftovers (rarely happens), warm them in the oven the next morning and plop a fried egg on top. Oh, my.

Stuffed Mushroom Caps
(from Chef Matt Weber at the Uptown Café in Louisville, Kentucky)

The Uptown Café, on the very eclectic Bardstown Road, is one of our favorite go-to restaurants and has been for years and years. We loved and were loved on by the original owner, Nancy Shepherd, God rest her soul. Her very fun and cute daughter, Kelley Ledford, now runs the Uptown. She graciously and patiently holds our window table when we run on "Hoagland time" (translation: a tad tardy). God bless her.

Nearly every time we visit the Uptown, we order the same thing: Caesar salad and their linguine with sesame chicken and broccoli with extra sauce. We get to where we crave it and have to dash over for a fix. When we're really hungry, we order up an appetizer. Same. One. Every. Time: stuffed mushroom caps. (Can you say, "Dogs of habit?" Likewise my friend Mary always orders the chicken piccata.) We pray whoever's plating the mushrooms will overserve the sauce, as we not only gobble up the stuffed mushrooms, we bathe our bread in the to-die-for sauce.

Gracious Chef Matt and Kelley are gifting us with the recipe. Bon appetit.

First, figure out how many of these mushroom caps you wish to make. Chef Matt likes to use silver dollar mushrooms, white, uncooked. Buy 1 or more pounds, according to how many you want. Clean and pull out the stems to prepare for stuffing.

Mushroom Stuffing
2½ pounds of Italian sausage
1¼ pound of ground chuck
½ pound of yellow onion, finely diced
1 oz. minced garlic
1 pound of goat cheese
1 cup bread crumbs

1½ teaspoon thyme
1 tablespoon basil
1 heaping teaspoon of pepper flakes
2–3 dashes of Tabasco
¼ bunch of flat leaf Italian parsley
Scant teaspoon each of salt and pepper

Directions

- Sautee sausage and ground chuck until browned and drain. Set aside.
- Sautee the onion and garlic together in olive oil until onions are translucent. Set aside.
- Combine all of the stuffing ingredients by hand or in a mixer with a paddle. Depending on mushroom size, it usually takes about ½ oz. of the stuffing to fill each mushroom. Yields: approximately 9¼ cups.

Stuff as many mushrooms as you'd like to serve your guests. Pop them in a 350-degree oven to bake while you make the sauce. For an appetizer order, John and I usually receive about six stuffed mushrooms on a salad-size plate, and they're happily sitting in the sauce. Oh, the sauce:

Brandy Cream Brown Sauce

2 cups heavy cream
1½ teaspoon chopped basil
4 oz. brandy, flamed
1 scant teaspoon each of salt and pepper
6 oz. of demi-glace

Directions

- Heat cream, basil, brandy, salt, and pepper until slightly thickened.

- Whisk in the demi-glace. Note: A demi-glace or brown sauce base can often be found at your local specialty stores. Yields: 2 cups.
- Uptown serves approximately ½ oz. of sauce per mushroom. Just make sure you have enough for the mushrooms and some to dip your French bread in, all the while erring on the generous side of serving the sauce.

My mouth is watering this very minute. I know where we're going for dinner tonight.

Third Stop: Understanding
(Friends from Bible Study)

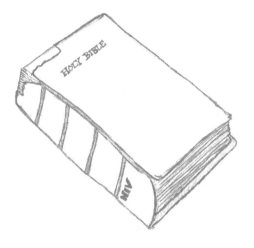

A party without cake is just a meeting.[1]
—Julia Child

I used to shy away from new beginnings. Think about graduating from the eighth grade, becoming a freshman in high school. Or bigger, graduating from high school and becoming a freshman in college. Right about the time you think you've arrived, you plunge right back down to the bottom rung of the ladder.

Slow to catch on, I up and transferred to a different college my sophomore year. I had to unearth what was cool all over *again*. A series of tests were thrown my way to see what I was made of.

Back in those days (no, I did not walk a mile in the snow to school), Wednesday nights at the University of Kentucky were *the* night to go out. A group of girls from my sorority met for Bible study in the living room of the Theta house. Guess which night? Oh yeah, Wednesday night. I learned from those *not* participating in the Bible study they dubbed those girls "the God Squad." There was *no way* I was going to be part of *that*. First test passed.

Where the real action on Wednesday nights took place was at Two Keys. This was not an elite club for higher education or tutoring. (Those of you from Lexington, Kentucky, or who are UK alums are howling your heads off.) Nope, Two Keys was and is a *bar*. And yes, many of us went, whether we were of age or not. Second test passed. (Please do not tattle on us to our children.)

Oh, but our most gracious Lord has a colossal sense of humor. He never gave up on me, even as rebellious and thick-skulled as I was back in college.

Nearly nine years later, it took four, count 'em four, invitations to get me to grace the doors of a Bible study class. Three of the invitations were from family members. One of those three came from my *mother-in-law*. Who says no to your mother-in-law? Uh, that would be me.

The fourth and final invitation arose from one of my peers. Her name is Susan (she's one of the Ya-Yas). She and I had our firstborns, Whitney and John Jr., two weeks apart.

Her invitation was especially interesting because it included the opportunity for us to tote our then two-year-olds to Bible study with us. Translation: free babysitting.

Bible Study Fellowship (BSF) has a children's program that goes on simultaneously with the adult program. Sold. I signed up.

Unsure of exactly what I was getting into, I pretended all was well. Even though I answered "no" three times, my uncomfortable yes led me into a whole new world. What was Bible study all about, anyway?

Equally unsure of what some of my other friends would think, I simply told them I was taking a class. Please tell me how you *hide* the fact you are taking a Bible study? Was I ashamed of it? Honestly, I don't know. Would this be like the God Squad? Please forgive me, Lord.

Friendly Encounters

Little did I know a Bible study would be the start of many friendships. I thought I was adding another win in the get-in-good-with-God column. Something to cross off my to-do list, the same way I would with working out and going shopping. I lived in the Bible Belt, after all, so going to a Bible study couldn't hurt. But I had no idea it would change things personally and relationally.

A few months into the Bible study, our teaching leader was taking us through the book of Genesis. All was well until she hit the part about Abraham readying to sacrifice Isaac (Genesis 22). As in his only son. As in the son he and his wife had been waiting for, for decades. Like nine and ten decades.

No way could I nor would I consider such a sacrifice. Even for the Big-G God. (I can picture Him shaking His head, saying. "Wow, this one's a tough nut to crack.")

Same teaching leader kept using words like *secular* and *spiritual*. It was BSF that opened my eyes. While I *thought* I was a Christian, indeed, I was *not*. It took another whole year for me to own up to it. Pride's a funny bird.

By this time, I was pregnant with our second child. One day at Seneca Park in Louisville, while waddling a couple of laps, I said to the Lord, "Okay, I give. I need to ask you into my heart and fess up a few things. Would that be okay?" The earth didn't shatter nor did time stand still, but I was happily becoming a new child of God.

In Bible study, my teacher taught us when we receive Christ, we become a new creation (2 Corinthians 5:17). That verse took on a whole new meaning for me from that day forward.

Several years and lots of Bible studies later, I was hooked. Now you can peg me as a God Squadder. Go ahead, I can take it.

Thankfully, my sister-friends from Bible study all realized if we weren't studying the Good Book, trouble would be a-brewin'. We realized we needed to be accountable to one another.

Harry Emerson Fosdick expounds on this idea of accountability: "The steady discipline of intimate friendship with Jesus results in men becoming like Him."[2] Friendship with Jesus is what keeps us showing up at Bible study. We want to know Him and understand Him better.

I'd heard grand things about Jane Chilton, the night-time BSF teaching leader, while I was in the morning BSF class. I graduated from the program and was on the hunt for a new class. Our church announced the very same Jane of BSF fame would be teaching a class that fall. Awesome. I enrolled as fast as I could.

My small group bonded immediately; Jane was (and is) a truly brilliant teacher, another gift from God. Never in a million years did I think Jane and I would become close friends and prayer warriors. God is beyond gracious.

I was in awe of Jane. Her fashionista style and obvious love for the Lord drew in women (and men in the night class) by the droves. Week after week, she not only looked like a million bucks (no one, I repeat no one, can sport an accessory or an outfit like Jane), but she delivered some of the best teachings I've ever heard.

While we were becoming acquainted, Jane and her husband, John, and my John and I were invited to go boating with mutual friends one night. We climbed aboard.

Jane and I went up on the top deck while the guys helped our captain navigate out of the marina. The wife of the captain was preparing hors d'oeuvres. Jane and I grabbed crackers with smoked salmon to take up with us.

Without warning, Jane sailed her cracker with salmon over the railing. The fish in the Ohio River have never been so grateful.

I said, "Oh dear, I haven't learned to eat smoked salmon, either."

Without missing a beat, Jane grabbed my cracker and chucked it overboard just before our hostess appeared up top with more appetizers. In all my years, I've never tried to suppress laughter welling up inside like that. I knew from that very sacrificial James Bond-like split-second action, Jane and I were going to be close-knit friends.

Gradually, our computers lit up with emails, ultimately finding us going out for lunch frequently. A. A. Milne couldn't have said it better: "It is more fun to talk with someone who doesn't use long, difficult words but rather short, easy words like 'What about lunch?'"[3] (One more fine "What? You too?")

One day, when Jane and I were lunching at one of our favorite Louisville haunts, Jack Fry's, she pulled out the big guns. She asked me if I'd pray about becoming a facilitator for her, as in joining her leadership team. As in having my own small group to lead and shepherd. Huh? Now she was messin' with me. Jane is gifted at pushing timid birds out of their nests.

This was my next uncomfortable yes. It would've been much easier to say, "Maybe later," or "Thanks, but no thanks." The funny thing I remember about my response was I left a qualifier in it: "Okay, well, yes, I'll be a facilitator for you, but I will *not* pray out loud." That lasted about one week.

Bible study has a way of blessing you with friends you've never had, young and old. My fellow facilitators were smart, and I loved learning from them. Over the years, the leadership team has grown and changed; we've studied different lessons, and we've added new members. We meet in Jane's home now. Of course, we have a name because by now, you know I love naming my friends.

Our name came from a scene in the movie *Young Frankenstein*. It's where Dr. Frankenstein is realizing something's a tad askew with his gargantuan creation. Seems Igor's mission to secure the brain of someone Dr. Frankenstein requested became botched. He accidentally sent the requested brain and its glass container crashing and burning onto the floor. The substitute Igor chose, much to Dr. Frankenstein's chagrin, was named "Abby something." It read: "Abby Normal," as in an abnormal brain, which Dr. Frankenstein had transplanted into their seven-and-a-half-foot-tall monster.

Picking up on the concept that we sister-friends were abnormal, "the Abbies," short for Abby Normal, were born. We somehow find comfort in this crazy culture in which we live, knowing we're foreigners on this earth.

The Hebrew name "Abbie" means "Father rejoiced" or "father's joy; gives joy." We Abbies definitely receive joy from one another.

On Bible study mornings, while driving to Jane's, I get excited about a verse that describes our time together perfectly. Hebrews 10:22a says, "Let us go right into the presence of God with sincere hearts fully trusting him" (NLT).

Upon arriving, we pull up a chair at Jane's beautiful dining room table. It's round, welcoming, and hugely conducive to meaningful discussion. A sacredness fills the room. I'm able to envision us going right into the presence of God. Prayer transports us there after we pile in with purses, pens, workbooks, iPads, and our Bibles, while our "sincere hearts fully trust Him." Each of these girls teaches me more from God's Word than I could ever discover on my own.

Many a morning before we arrive for Bible study, Jane will shoot us a text saying, "Be on time. Biscuits will be ready at ten o'clock." Sister-friend, these aren't just any biscuits. These are Jane's perfection of a recipe from Lynn's Paradise Café, a former favorite in Louisville. I call them "Bible Study Biscuits" to sound more spiritual. ("Lucifer Loaves" would be more apropos.)

When served up at Lynn's Paradise Café (now closed, sadly), these biscuits undid many a patron, not to mention a plethora of celebrities, Oprah included. Jane whisks the biscuits right out of the oven, their tops beautifully browned, accompanying them with creamy butter and homemade blackberry jam and fresh fruit. We've decided the fruit cancels out the calories of the biscuits.

It's astonishing how our attendance improves with the biscuits. Our Lord is shaking His head. Again. (Recipe's at the end of this chapter. Take a gander at the ingredients, but never reveal them to your guests.)

Cake also plays a large role with the Abbies. Jane's pound cake started the ball rolling years ago. (Do *not* miss this recipe, either. It's on my website.) Then we added experiments from most of the bakeries in town, including Sam's Club, even trying local, individual cake bakers. (While black polka dots on white cake are cute, the black icing wreaks havoc with your teeth and tongue, causing you to look like you just stepped out of a horror film. Just a head's up.)

In Their Own Words

Week in and week out, my Abbies experience the all-surpassing power of God's Word seeping into our souls, thanks to Bible study, a few biscuits, and sometimes a slice of cake. It's because these are my Understanding Friends, as I like to call them. They understand me. And together we seek to understand the Word of God. It's a type of friendship that digs deep.

I'm dying for you to meet and hear from the Abbies. Background-wise, a few of us go back to BSF leadership days. A few were on staff at Southeast Christian Church in Louisville, Kentucky and most of us were on the Women's Council. These friends have shown me what it means to be accountable; to serve others; to be cement-like; to think globally; and when friends comprise a fruit salad.

Being Accountable

Lynn Reece, who's a spiritual mom to all of us, and who also leads us on many occasions, prays the Lord will call her heavenward while she's teaching Bible study. She's dead serious (pun intended).

Her Southern drawl, thanks to her upbringing in a small Georgia town, enhances her teaching. Her newest idea for us each Christmas, besides hosting a brunch accompanied by her to-die-for cheese grits (yes, recipe's on my website), was for us to come to her favorite things party. This is our new tradition.

Lynn instructs us to bring one of our favorite things for each Abbie, wrapped. Then we must explain how you cannot live without this item. Items have ranged from the good ol' "as seen on TV" products, to books, to foodie goodies, to lovely lotions. We not only go home with fabulous gifts, we learn a lot each time. Do try this with your friends. (Our daughter-in-love, LT, does this with her friends too, proving it's a thumbs-up for all ages.)

As of this writing, Lynn's teaching three classes at three different churches each week while attending our Wednesday class. Small detail: She's in her seventh decade. Lynn has taught me many things, including accountability. She likes to talk about how it changed her life:

Prior to serving as a director of women's ministry, I'd never led a group of so many women, so I promptly registered for a conference in California to learn how to do women's ministry.

A director from a church in Oregon told me, "Go home and get yourself an accountability partner. Find someone you can trust, someone you can bare your soul to, someone you can scream and holler about your job to, and someone with whom you can be friends."

I asked God to lead me to the right person. He did. Surprisingly, it wasn't who I expected. This gal and I met weekly for thirteen years and also did Bible study together.

Our friendship grew as we began to share our hearts, our hurts, our passions, and our struggles. What started simply as a person for me to discuss ministry issues with, without using my husband as a sounding board (God bless him), led to so much more.

I remember a remark my friend made early into our friendship. As we shared our prayer requests with each other every week, she said, "This is the first time in my life I have someone who I know is praying for me every day." Wow! Do you know what a blessing that is?

I gleaned three lessons from having an accountability partner: First, I had to reach out and ask her to be my accountability partner. Neither of us knew what to expect. Second, we found out it took work. Neither of us had been this open and honest with any other woman. We had to learn to trust each other unconditionally. Third, good friendships take quantity and quality time together.

We laughed, we cried, and we grew as friends and as women of faith. Sadly, my special accountability friend soon discovered she had pancreatic cancer. Then we had a different road to travel. This was a major detour for us. In less than a year, God would take her home. Was there a deep loss? Absolutely.

I miss her every day. I miss being able to call her on the phone and run something by her. I miss her sweet, gregarious personality. And yet I'm so grateful for the time we had. I wouldn't have missed it for anything.

Because of that foundational relationship, coupled with God's guiding hand, our women's ministry not only survived but thrived.

From what Lynn learned, this translated into each of the Abbies holding one another accountable. Thank you, Lynn.

If one of us can't make it to Bible study, we're responsible for reporting our whereabouts. We're blissfully assured we're missed when we can't be with one another. The writing of this book, for example, has kept me from meeting the Abbies on many Wednesdays, but I still report in and can happily say I feel their prayers.

Serving Others

One of Lynn's indispensable staffers was Gwen Paten. I was blessed to work with Gwen on several women's events at SEC. I was immediately drawn to her magnetic personality. (You saw her in action on our first stop with the book club.)

I call Gwen "Gwennie." Always have.

Nothing flusters Gwennie, while minuscule things wreck me. When she was on staff at SEC, she could throw together a function for five or fifty or five thousand women. No problemo.

She taught me what it means to serve others. My first experience of living out Zephaniah 3:9 came thanks to Gwennie: "Then I will purify the lips of the peoples, that all of them may call on the name of the Lord and *serve Him shoulder to shoulder*" (emphasis mine).

Gwennie can and will do anything for anyone. Her current job has brought her hat decorating fame, just to name one of her many talents. Here in Kentucky Derby territory, this is a claim to fame we do not take lightly. All the while, her employers smile with glee.

I want you to see a more serious side of Gwen. You'll be amazed at how she handled a shocking detour that befell her and her husband, Mike. Mike died of cancer only thirty-three days after being diagnosed. Let that sink in a minute. I'm still shaking my head, reading these words, many years later.

The Abbies began meeting soon after Mike's funeral. We thought it was our duty to watch over Gwen, when it's actually been her blessing us in a thousand ways every Wednesday.

While Mike's death could've derailed all of us, the Lord's presence encircled us and comforted us, enabling us to walk alongside Gwennie. This was an uncomfortable yes for all of us, but together, we helped each other. Here's what Gwennie has to say about navigating those rough waters:

> I never imagined my participation in Women's Bible studies, Weekend Church, Adult Bible Fellowship Class, and a Home Bible Fellowship Group would prepare me for one of the most difficult challenges I'd ever have to face. The friendships that grew out of these groups forged an impenetrable fortress.
>
> When the docs discovered the cancer was in Mike's bones, it had already spread throughout his body; our friends dove in head first. They walked us through what would be our most devastating farewell.

For thirty-three days, from diagnosis to Mike's unthinkable death, he and I read God's Word and several devotionals, posting scripture on the hospital walls, praying for God's will to be done. These same friends from church visited us, bringing treats to eat, praying, hugging, and crying with us. The Lord graciously blessed us with beautiful moments of closure before Mike went to be with Him.

Facing each new day in my new normal was anything but normal. What's in your mind, heart, and soul is what comes to you first. My favorite passages of scripture are from Psalm 46 and Jeremiah 29:11.

I believe God administers what I call "holy anesthesia" to help us grieve and endure the pain. He also gifts us with Christian friends to journey with, greatly lightening our burden.

I love those two words from Gwennie: "holy anesthesia." With it, as in the Word of God, my sister-friend, we *can* do life together. Gwennie's servant's heart has influenced the Abbies to follow suit on many occasions. We praise you, Lord.

Being Cement-Like

Another sister-friend in the Abbies is Betsy Heady. She and I met through our leader, Jane.

Betsy married David (thanks to Jane playing Cupid). He's in the lighting business and, as an added bonus, has transformed our last two homes. It's all about the light, but that's a story for another day.

Betsy and I affectionately call each other "the Other EMH" because we have the exact same initials. Yes, we are like little schoolgirls.

Betsy's an incredible decorator. Her home, her attire, everything about her is always put together, effortlessly. She was the first Joanna Gaines before Joanna was a household name.

Eight years ago, Betsy got the phone call no parent ever wants to receive. This was a major detour. Her son, Paul, a police officer, nearly forty years old, died in a bicycle accident.

Betsy is a picture of 2 Corinthians 1:3–4, which says, "Praise be to the God and Father of our Lord Jesus Christ, the Father of compassion and the God of all comfort, who comforts us in all our troubles, so that we can comfort those in any trouble with the comfort we ourselves receive from God" (NLT). Over the years, Betsy's met many a parent in a hospital whose child has just died. Seeing her minister to these grieving families time after time takes your breath away.

Over the past eighteen years, Betsy has led small groups of women in Bible studies. She says she's still blown away by the depth of friendships that develop in these groups. She explains:

> I don't know of any other venue that has the power to cement relationships like the gathering of believers studying the Word of God and praying together. Relationships cemented in this way stand the test of time, rejoicing together in our victories, and weeping together in the storms.
>
> My husband, David, and I witnessed an eye-opening visual of the power, or lack thereof, of cement from a visit to Haiti in 2010 after an earthquake hit where my in-laws are missionaries. The devastation was a clear picture of the importance of good cement.Most of Haiti's structures were built with inferior cement (more sand than cement), rendering them weak and vulnerable to storms and earthquakes. In Matthew 7:24, Jesus teaches that the wise man built his house on the rock. His house did not fall when the storms came.

The rock represents a solid foundation that begins with a personal relationship with Jesus Christ, the only good cement. He gives us strength to withstand the storms of life, coming out victorious on the other side. Part of the miraculous power He provides is the love and friendship of other believers that have cemented our hearts through Bible study.

The storm we experienced allowed us to see a live performance of our Bible study friends being the hands and feet of Jesus. I will never be able to erase the memory of walking into our home after leaving the hospital where my son died and being overwhelmed by so many friends gathered together to grieve with us. They not only provided nourishment for our broken hearts, but our kitchen was covered with food, and meals continued for days. Sometimes consoling words can't be spoken, but God's people were there, showing us love and support in ways that cannot be explained.

The most tangible blessing is found in the family of God in our Bible study. Jesus Christ has been the cement for all these relationships, and for this we are forever grateful.

I think friendship and faith in Jesus Christ is the best cement there is. And with that, all the Abbies shout a resounding "Amen!" President Woodrow Wilson said, "Friendship is the only cement that will ever hold the world together."[4] Sister-friend, may this concept be cemented in our brains.

Thinking Globally

Another of our Abbies bears a unique distinction. Her name is Olivia Kirtley. One of her many talents is she's an entertainer extraordinaire. Over the years, when we've all hosted parties, either together or individually, it's Olivia's closet we run to for the most beautiful serving pieces anyone could hope to use.

We also refer to Olivia as our genius friend. Just by watching her, we find ourselves challenged to be globally minded. Besides being a wife, a mom (to three boys), a grandmother, and a fabulous cook, she's an accountant by trade. She ran a local company in Louisville for years. Then she became head of the CPAs in the United States. Then she became the vice deputy (vice president) for the CPAs in the world. Soon after that, she became the first female president of that organization, known as the International Federation of Accountants (IFAC).

Wait 'til you hear about her inauguration into that role: For her very first meeting in her new role at the IFAC, she'd be speaking in Italy.

In the Vatican.

With the pope.

What?

Oh, and this gets better. Her talk needed to be in Italian. Incidentally, she learned this petite detail three days prior to the event. (You can see how very much we have in common.)

Often, I'll text Olivia and say, "Where in the world are you?" And I mean it quite literally. With her travels all over the world to many cities and countries we've never heard of, she often offers us lessons in geography.

The Abbies recently discovered many people across the pond refer to Olivia as "Madam Kirtley." We decided a red-carpet welcome was in order for her next visit to our Bible study.

That particular week, bolts of red felt were a steal at Jo-Ann Fabrics. We covered Jane's hallway with the felt, creating quite the red-carpet runway. Each Abby stood at attention, flanking both sides of the carpet, ready with "the wave" once Olivia stepped off the elevator. Yes, our time together in Bible study is not only sacred, it's downright silly.

One of Olivia's favorite stories in her travels happened on a small island nation off the southern tip of India…

I first went to Sri Lanka with five other businesspeople to help after it had been struck by a tsunami. We went armed with donations, our mission being to rebuild businesses that had been destroyed, hoping to allow people to be able to support their families again. That was in 2005.

This time, in 2015, I was returning as president of the IFAC. I was to visit government officials, professionals, and business leaders, to talk about how professional accountancy organizations could support their ambitious economic growth goals under a newly elected president.

Secretly, I was most excited to see everyone I'd met before, particularly to see what had become of the girls and boys at the orphanages we had helped.

I discovered an email from Charmaine, one of the directors of the orphanages we had helped. Charmaine told me she'd read the program for an upcoming meeting and realized I was their keynote speaker. Charmaine works for the World Bank and would be attending the same meeting.

Over our years of friendship and support of the orphanages, we were totally unaware of our business connection. I quickly replied and asked if we could spend the weekend visiting the new girls' and boys' homes built following the tsunami.

Upon arrival, the years melted away. Seeing the children's gorgeous smiles, along with the large sign they'd made, "Welcome Back Ms. Olivia," was over-the-top wonderful.

I instantly recognized a few of the girls, now ten years older, beautiful, and mature. They hugged me and gave me a tour of their new home and their own rooms.

After much conversation and laughter, they gathered to sing to me, proudly wearing beautiful long skirts that Hopeful Hearts Foundation had sent them for Christmas the year before. Although many of the girls didn't speak English, they'd worked hard to learn the songs in English. These were songs of love, faith, and hope, plus a surprise ending of them singing "My Old Kentucky Home." My heart was ready to burst!

When they wanted to hear from me, I wondered, "What advice did I have? What could I tell them?" I already knew they had the most important things in life: love, faith, and deep friendships. My message that day was simple: Hold on to your faith, pursue your dreams, and never forget what you already have—friends to do life with, no matter what, for now and forever.

This story is one of many Olivia has shared with us, proving the Lord is working all over the world. He showed us via Olivia how we must think and pray globally with better understanding in many arenas.

I'd be remiss if I didn't tell you about another Bible study group I've been blessed to attend. It was only recently that my friend, Mary, came up with a name for us. (You'll meet Mary on our fifth stop.) Thanks to her creativity, our Tuesday group is now known as "Blessings on Burlington (B on B)".

These precious gals come from many different churches. Our hostess is Susan, the same Susan who got me involved in my very first Bible study. She lives on Burlington Avenue, thence our moniker. You know this makes me so very happy.

Several years ago, Susan asked if I'd like to do a Bible study in her home. I was committed to another group at the time, but a window of opportunity soon opened up. This was another uncomfortable yes for me to accept because we weren't really certain about how this would all shake out.

We prayed about who to invite. Twenty names popped in our heads. We mailed twenty invitations, and ten gals showed up. We've evolved over the years, now numbering to twenty-two.

When Friends Comprise a Fruit Salad

One of many lovely additions to B on B is Anna Bates. Anna and I go way back to high school in Lexington. We reconnected at church a few years ago, stunned to find one another in church. Quite the comical "What? You too?"

Anna knows no strangers and dubs her friends "a fruit salad of friendships." Let's see why:

> "Love me and love my people" is the calling the Lord tenderly knitted into my life. Thankfully, with the calling came the blessing, and I've not met a stranger. Wherever I am, I'm on red alert for when the Lord wants to introduce me to someone new. It's also true the Lord's called me to walk through life *without* the company of my sisters, having lost each of them and my mother much earlier along my way.
>
> At this intersection of love and loss, the Lord has taught me the eternal value of relationship and has provided deep, soul-bearing friendships. They often arrive in unexpected places like a dental clinic in Kenya, a Bible study, or even behind a service desk. Each time, I'm blessed with a renewed sense of wonder at the vastness of the Lord since we're all made in His image.

> The Lord says in Proverbs 17:17a, "A friend loves at all times," and in Matthew 7:20, "Thus, by their fruit you will recognize them." He has richly blessed me with a bountiful fruit salad of friendships.
>
> Lord, thank you for the gift of sister-friends. I pray you'll make me known by the fruit of love: loving you and loving others.

Sister-friend, next time we're with our friends, may we picture ourselves as a big, beautiful fruit salad. This fun visual implies how very good we all are for each other. Thank you, Anna.

Inspiration to Go

Understanding is our shared activity on this stop, largely from God's Word pouring over us like holy anesthesia, as Gwennie calls it, providing a cement-like foundation. Psalm 119:130 portrays our time together: "The unfolding of your words gives light; it gives understanding to the simple."

Where do I start, you ask? Pray about which God Squad you'll join, or better yet, start one yourself. How about checking with your church or inviting your neighbors or your friends?

We've gleaned many benefits from Bible study, including
- making new friends,
- gleaning new insight into God's Word,
- understanding the Bible (and therefore Christ) better,
- having the opportunity to teach children what you're learning,
- discovering your time together is therapeutic from the fellowship that will develop,
- being accountable to others (this may not sound like a benefit, but believe me, it is so good for you),
- serving others,

- experiencing the Word cementing your relationships together,
- thinking and praying globally, and
- observing how the sacred can also be silly with your sister-friends (e.g., Lucifer Loaves, red carpet welcome, and favorite things party).

I ran across the perfect quote to end this chapter with, by Octavius Winslow, a nineteenth-century evangelical preacher from England, on what he thinks about the Bible:

Let me believe it firmly,

deal with it reverently,

read it devoutly, and

walk in its divine precepts holily, and

do all in my power to give it to all who may not possess, as I do,

this heavenly chart,

this divine compass,

this unerring light in the soul's solemn travel to eternity.

Before we travel onward, toward eternity, sister-friend, you gotta meet the Butter Babes.

Motivation-for-Getting-to-Bible-Study Biscuits
(from Jane Chilton; gluten-free option also included)

I mentioned that Jane texts the Abbies many a Wednesday morning with, "Biscuits are in the oven. They'll be ready at 10." I'd love to tell you we dash to Bible study, super promptly, week after week, but many of us run on the late side. Like Oreos dangling before the racing pigs at the Kentucky State Fair, these biscuits make the Abbies race to Bible study.

These biscuits were made famous and inhaled by thousands of customers when Lynn's Paradise Café was open. *Southern Living* featured the café's owner, Lynn, and many of her recipes annually.

Lynn defined eclectic, from the décor to the menu to the gift shop. Many a year, I'd trek there purely to shop for stocking stuffers. (Shhh, don't tell my children.)

If these biscuits work in my kitchen, they'll work in yours. Make them for company, but remember, don't reveal the highly nutritious ingredients. Your secret is safe with me.

Ingredients
    4 cups White Lily flour
    4 teaspoons baking powder
    1¼ teaspoon salt
    1 teaspoon baking soda
    ⅔ cup butter (Lynn's recipe calls for shortening)
    1½ cups buttermilk
    1 cup heavy cream
    2 tablespoons butter, melted

Directions
- Heat oven to 425 degrees.
- In a large bowl, sift together the flour, baking powder, salt, and baking soda.

- Cut the butter into the flour mixture with a pastry blender until it's the size of small peas. (I don't own a pastry blender, nor do I know what one is; I just use a fork and a knife, to which most chefs are now visibly horrified.)
- Pour in the buttermilk and cream. Fold and blend together with a rubber spatula. The dough will be very sticky and wet.
- Grease a 9-inch-square baking pan with nonstick spray. Spoon the batter into the pan, and even it out with the rubber spatula. Dust your hands with flour, and lightly pat the dough until it is even; press it into the corners.
- Using a floured table knife or pastry cutter, cut through the dough to make 9 or 16 square biscuits. Brush with melted butter, and bake for 35 minutes. Test to make sure the biscuits are done by carefully lifting the crust of the middle biscuit and poking the bread underneath. The bread should spring back when pressed. If the dough still seems wet and spongy, put the biscuits back in the oven and bake for an additional 5 minutes or until firm.
- Remove the biscuits from the oven, letting them rest for 5 minutes before cutting.
- Makes nine 3-inch or sixteen 2-inch biscuits.

(For a gluten-free option, Jane makes a smaller portion for our friend, Betsy, using gluten-free flour. We prefer Pamela's All-Purpose Flour, Gluten-Free, Artisan Blend, Non-Dairy.)

Fourth Stop: Laughing (Friends from Butter: The Butter Babes)

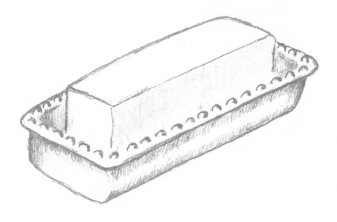

With enough butter, anything is good.[1]
—Julia Child

Five friends were crammed in a corner booth in Panera. High noon. No spare chairs.

It was fall, and Panera's autumn squash soup was clearly irresistible to half the city. Something was amiss, however. In that corner booth, my normally chatty friends were silent. Odder still, ten for ten of our shoulders were shaking.

Suddenly, a squeak eked out of Nancy, followed by some sputtering by Bonnie, chortling by Judy, howling by Fay, and gasping for air from yours truly.

The explosion could not be prevented. It erupted right then and there, from that little corner booth.

The cause? The reading of *The Butter Bride,* written by my cousin, Bonnie. No other piece of literature has ever had this effect on us, before or since.

Bonnie became inspired to write *The Butter Bride* after attending a wedding in North Carolina, where she saw a sculpture, strongly resembling the bride, which was perched on a table at the reception.

I want you, sister-friend to be in on this. Here's how Bonnie began her story:

> I'm here to tell ya, there is such a thing as an ugly bride. Last August, I saw her—in North Carolina—standing in the basement of the Mount Pleasant Baptist Church after a candlelight wedding ceremony in the middle of a white-hot afternoon.
>
> I don't mean she was a bit homely or bless-her-heart ugly. I'm here to tell you she was run-to-mama, nightmare, gotta sleep-with-the-lights-on ugly. She was scare-the-baby and close-the-shutters ugly.

Ah yes, Bonnie captured our attention with that. We were on the edge of our seats, while she continued about the deacons carrying this thing out into the reception hall:

> The slender, elegant bride wore a long gown scalloped with beaded lace trim around the bottom, with pillowy folds of satin as smooth as the fondant icing on the three-tiered wedding cake. Her golden hair was patted smooth on the sides and fastened in a wreath on top of her head. Victorian curls spiraled down her neck and teased her shoulders. Her train was embroidered like intricate carvings of amber.

In the middle of the room, there she stood atop a round table intended for wedding gifts. Sunshine radiant, high cheekbones, perfect teeth peeking through full smiling lips. She looked imperial? Regal? A work of art so stunning, I stood speechless, like my feet were nailed to the floor and my brain cells had dissolved in the heat. She, that life-size replica of the bride, who was at the time upstairs having pictures made, was petite—just over five feet tall—and sculpted entirely from butter. Virginal Land O'Lakes. Cultured. Straight from the freezer into the furnace of a sultry afternoon, perfumed with hope, and hot as newlywed passion.

Four out of four of our hands were over our mouths, our eyes as big as our soup bowls. Here's where the bride has her denouement (buckle your seat belt):

Right away, the 106 degree heat index caused condensation to form on the butter bride. After her sequester in the walk-in refrigerator prior to the reveal, heat brought moisture to the surface of the sculpture in less than ten minutes. Before our eyes, modifications and alterations in her appearance began to surface. Her expression changed from one of serene bliss to that of a jaundiced, aging woman whose countenance morphed bitter with tiny lines forming, while a mass of sweat beads appeared on her once smooth and creamy complexion. On the forehead and the round cheeks brushed with pink blush, a mass of droplets grew larger 'til they spilled over themselves, making tiny streams—from her eyes, her ears, her nose—rivuletting down her ample and youthful cleavage, causing her to sag before her time. Her summer blue eyes—tinted with cornflower blue eyeshadow—turned the color of blooming ragweed; she cried yellow unsalted tears, this bride with butter boogers.[2]

Ewww.

Recovery from said reading took an inordinate amount of time. Certain we'd be evicted from Panera for such behavior, we were surprised people went right along slurping their soup. This was not unusual for us. We were accustomed to laughing together and cracking up at the most inconvenient times. In fact, our group laughter started long before that day in Panera.

Friendly Encounters

Our little group of five women have been friends for years, but we'd never had a moniker to call our own. Our lack of a name after all this time was of great distress to me, until that hilarious moment (many, many, *many* moments, actually) where we couldn't stop ourselves from laughing. You know when the harder you try to stifle the laugh, the challenge becomes exponentially more difficult?

We suddenly began rattling off one butter phrase after another: "Well, butter my derriere [keepin' it clean, here] and call me a biscuit," and "Fry me in butter and call me a catfish" (we have a bounty of catfish in Kentucky; they're known as "bottom feeders." Ewww again), plus "I'll love you more than butter" and our current favorite, "I don't want it unless it's fried, covered in butter, and speaks with a Southern accent."

We calmed down a tad. Bonnie read more. The more she read, the more we learned about butter sculpting, not just of brides, but of everything you'd *never* think of from contests at the Iowa and Minnesota state fairs, only further multiplying our laughter.

A sudden "aha" surfaced:

"I've got it!" I cried, still wiping tears and mascara away from my eyes. "We need to call ourselves the Butter Babes."

Boom. The Butter Babes were born. Butter our perpetual theme. All was well, once again, in the Panera Bread Company.

The Butter Babes comprise a circle of five: Judy, Bonnie, Nancy, Fay, and yours truly.

Since that momentous day we were named, we've been on a lifelong quest to procure every variety of butter (Kerrygold Irish butter a favorite), turkey-shaped butter for Thanksgiving, Christmas tree-shaped butter for Yuletide, eggs made out of butter and delivered on Easter by Judy, butter rum mints, body butter, items in the color of butter yellow, soaps made with butter, butter dishes, recipes with butter, quotes about butter, and, well, you get our mission. It's a deep one, at that.

Ah, but these dear friends are sincerely deep spiritually and laugh-your-head-off funny. You'll be hearing from them (and from some of their daughters at a later stop), giving you a sneak peek into our crazy capers, which can easily morph into capers you can have with your own friends.

Charles Dickens said, "There is nothing in the world so irresistibly contagious as laughter and good humour."[3] Ah, yes, and we can take that laughter one step further: "A joyful heart is good medicine" (Proverbs 17:22a ESV).

Being with the Butter Babes brings forth pure joy, laughter, and cheaper-than-therapy fellowship. Our gatherings, while challenging to accomplish because of our busy schedules, are the equivalent of receiving a healthy booster shot. (That's the good medicine part.)

Unlike the Abbies from our last stop, the Butter Babes are not in Bible study together. We all attend different ones. Many times, we share what we're learning, which makes for a different side to sacred, sister-friend time. Our fellowship flows, whether sitting around a table or going on a road trip.

This has proven itself true as we've journeyed together through sad times and happy times. One of our more serious detours lasted for eight long months when Tommy, our friend Fay's husband, was on the heart transplant list. This was a hugely uncomfortable yes, but together, the Babes prayed feverishly for Tommy who, praise the Lord, is doing well today, with his original heart.

Romans 12:10b hones in on where our friendships play out: "Be good friends who love deeply; practice playing second fiddle" (The Message). The Butter Babes could care less who the first fiddle may be; we're content to play second, third, and fourth fiddle any day.

We do, however, have one Babe we've had the pleasure of naming "Butter Superior," perhaps placing her at first fiddle. Her name is Judy Russell. Those of you who know her are laughing, knowing Judy never, emphasis on *never*, wants to be in the spotlight. We simply thrust her in it, anyway.

A few years ago, Judy was about to have a spectacular (as in milestone) birthday. The Babes felt it only appropriate to make her queen for the weekend, kidnapping her to an obscure location. (We thought it prudent to obtain permission first from her husband, Bob.)

We took her on the road trip of all road trips, to a castle in Versailles. I'd love to tell you it was Versailles, as in France, but there's a real-live castle in Versailles, Kentucky.

I've called it Cinderella's castle for years. When our boys were little, we'd pass this castle on the way to my parents' home in Lexington. I always told our boys Cinderella lived there. That's either cultivating an imagination or full-on lying to one's child. You be the judge.

The Babes' time at the castle evaporated all too quickly. Each event we shared, including a melt-in-your-mouth five-course meal, was a delightful discovery. We spent a fun-filled evening feting Judy with cake, laughter, and different crowns for each portion of the day-turned-evening. At one point, we played a game called Origin that Nancy unpacked for us. The game, with Nancy at its helm, nearly brought down the castle from our howling.

Henry Nouwen's words capture our evening: "Joy and laughter are the gifts of living in the presence of God and trusting that tomorrow is not worth worrying about."[4] Happy to report there wasn't one ounce of worry going around the game table that evening.

Another one of the Butter Babes is like a big sister to me. Her name is Bonnie Johnson. (Oh yes, the author of *The Butter Bride*.) We're cousins by marriage, even though most people think we're sisters. Our "What? You too?" moment began when I was but five years old.

I believe it was my prophetic challenge that united Bonnie and Steve in holy matrimony. The first time I met Bonnie, she came to stay with us one weekend for a UK football game. I loved watching her curl her hair and put on makeup, all big-girl stuff. I became her little shadow.

Sadly, the weekend came to an end. She and Steve were returning to Owensboro, and I pouted profusely. Bonnie noticed and asked what was wrong.

I simply said, "Well, I'm so sad to see you leave because I know I'll *never* see you again. Steve brings a different girl here every weekend."

That's probably about the time Mother registered me for finishing school.

Bonnie and Steve continued to date; they got married and are living happily ever after right up the street. I was in their wedding, their kids were in our wedding, and our kids have been in their kids' weddings.

It was Bonnie who bought me my first pair of blue jeans. I was smitten.

I remember recipes she wrote out for me had scripture verses on them. She was sowing seeds of faith, which took years for me to pick up on. Praise the Lord, she and Steve never gave up on me. They loved me from afar through my difficult teenager years and my wild college years.

It warms my heart and makes me think of 1 John 3:1, how they took care of me and later our young family all these years: "See what great love the Father has lavished on us, that we should be called children of God!"

Since Bonnie and Steve moved to Louisville, Bonnie's been dubbed the Martha Stewart of our family. My friends recognize a "Bonnie bow" on any package. Many of us have been known to swing by Bonnie's house, present her with a gift (for someone else, no less), and watch her whip up one of her gorgeous bows.

Not long after so many of us requested bows, Bonnie came up with the brilliant idea of hosting a Christmas wrapping party. This, sister-friend, is one of the most fun things the Butter Babes do; we call it our favorite Christmas tradition. You can easily do this with your friends.

All year long, Bonnie hunts down a surplus of supplies for wrapping gifts, creating quite a smorgasbord of ribbon and wrapping paper. At the Christmas wrapping party, Bonnie plops a tarp over their pool table, and each Butter Babe moves in, claiming their spot. Armed with scissors, miles of scotch tape, and piles of gifts to be wrapped, we settle in for the afternoon, Christmas music serenading us from afar.

Since Fay is our youthful one, she often finds a place to sit on the floor and wraps. We wiser, older ones (don't believe that) know we couldn't get up from the floor if our lives depended on it.

We solve multiple problems, pray for people, and often make gift boxes for those in need. Every year brings forth a different opportunity.

The other smart thing this tradition has taught us is to be ready early for Christmas with your gifts. Take heed, fellow procrastinators. When you go home from a wrapping party, your tree looks more beautiful with these packages underneath, and you find you're able to enjoy and savor the season a little more each year.

In Their Own Words

As I think about the Butter Babes, I realize that while we're having a lot of fun together and laughing a lot, they've taught me specific lessons: friendship doesn't have to be hard work; laughing and crying are good for the soul; the table bonds friends; and faithful friends make the best of friends.

Friendship Doesn't Have to Be Hard Work

Because Bonnie was my first teacher in all things cool, it only seems fitting to start with a profound truth she taught me: Friendship doesn't have to be hard work. In fact, the more fun you have, the easier it is to bond.

Bonnie makes everything seem easy. And that's the best part. As you read more of her writing, you'll find new explanations about the Butter Babes none of us could have possibly come up with. Don't miss the jaw-dropping math about us, either:

> You may falsely assume the term "Butter Babes" refers to groupies of a famous Savannah kitchen maven or a group of portly women who devour butter in all its glory. We are not.
>
> I'd like to tell you we are all slim with healthy eating habits and buns of iron. We are not.
>
> You may wonder if we are a group of advocates for inedible benefits of butter, like easing minor burn pain on a forearm accidentally blistered when it came in contact with a hot oven rack or after holding a match so long it burns your fingers. We are not.
>
> What we *are* is a quintet of women of varying ages with similar concerns. Collectively, we've been married for two hundred years and have eleven children, fifteen grandchildren, oceans of love, and acres of laughter. We encourage and listen to each other. We pray for each other. We celebrate birthdays; after all, our ages total more than three hundred years. We celebrate ideas and share tears. Three of us are published authors, and we solicit the opinions of the rest of us.

Why, then, would we embrace the name Butter Babes with such enthusiasm and nurture it for over twenty years? We feel almost legendary when an acquaintance asks, "Are you one of the Butter Babes?" and we answer affirmatively.

That we embrace butterdom and continue to refer to ourselves as the Butter Babes has little to do with our babedom or the ninety pounds of molded butter used to form a representation of the bride by a certain caterer. What it means to us is the grand friendship that binds us through imperfect times and jubilates us in victorious ones.

Butter oils our days and flavors our lives. We grow buttercups in the garden and order butter on popcorn at the movies.

No matter how much butter we incorporate into our lives, it all pales in comparison to how much the Butter Babes love and are loved on by each other. It would probably just melt your heart. Really.

Bonnie melts all of our hearts in a myriad of ways each time we're together. She's forever introducing us to something new, whether it's from a new book, a foodie dish she's concocted, or bonding the Babes with more sweet memories.

Laughing and Crying Are Good for the Soul

Konrad Lorenz, a Nobel Prize winner and scientist, defined our bonding: "Heartily laughing together at the same thing forms an immediate bond, much as enthusiasm for the same ideal does. Finding the same thing funny is not only a friendship, but very often the first step to its formation."[5]

Laughter is what I think of when I think of this next Babe. I spoke of her on our first stop, and now you get to become acquainted with Nancy the Hugging Evangelist. Nobody gives hugs like Nancy Aguiar (those of you who've been on the receiving end are nodding).

Nancy the Hugging Evangelist also happens to be crazy comical. When I see her name flash across my cell phone, I start laughing before I ever answer. My howling causes her to howl, and we howl together for a few minutes before uttering a word. She exemplifies a favorite Southernism: she is "three gallons of crazy in a two-gallon bucket."

We also have a borderline-sick addiction to alliteration. "What? You too?" Our all-time winning phrase occurred when the Butter Babes Belatedly Celebrated Bonnie's Birthday at the Bountiful Bread Bakery. Come on now, who could make that up?

As fast as we can be thrown into fits of laughter, Nancy can just as quickly melt into a puddle of tears over someone struggling in their faith or over something from God's Word. Her compassion for others, coupled with her love for the Lord and His Word, is one of my favorite attributes about Nancy.

Nancy's had several different careers. Over the years, she's been a caregiver for several of our friends' mothers, my own included. On days when Nancy was headed to the nursing home to sit with Mother, I took great relief knowing she was going to have a fabulous day.

Mother was a glass-half-empty gal, bordering on being depressed much of the time. Nancy was the prescription she needed. When Mother went to be with the Lord, Nancy preached her funeral. I know. Not many friends would do that.

Nancy's trust in the Lord is perfectly described in 1 Peter 1:8–9 (NLT): "You love him even though you have never seen him. Though you do not see him now, you trust him; and you rejoice with a glorious, inexpressible joy. The reward for trusting him will be the salvation of your souls."

While I maintain it's her humor that'll cure what ails you, her sincere love for the Lord and His Word will refresh you. One day, I asked Nancy to explain why she weeps over God's Word. I so desire to cultivate that kind of passion. Savor Nancy's answers:

There are so many reasons why I love the Word of God. It teaches, convicts, directs, and refreshes me. Joy springs forth from hearing the Author speak to me personally. He and His Word are my dearest friends.

Other reasons are rooted in the scriptures themselves:

- God's Word is eternal (Isaiah 40:8). My best friend lives forever.
- God's Word is truth (John 17:17). My best friend can't lie.
- God's Word is transformational (Ezekiel 36:26). My best friend makes me a better me.
- God's Word is power (Hebrews 4:12). My best friend is powerful.
- God's Word is light (Psalm 119:105). My best friend lights my world.

Ephesians 2:8–9 sums it up best: "God saved you through faith as an act of kindness. You had nothing to do with it. Being saved is a gift from God. It's not the result of anything you've done, so no one can brag about it" (God's Word Translation). No other friend could do such a thing for us. What a gift.

Nancy's friendship with the Lord is contagious to everyone around her. She believes one way to become better acquainted with Jesus is to surround yourself with people in ministry. Watch how Judy does this—a great example to follow.

The Table Bonds Friends

Judy's been married to Bob for fifty-plus years. With their large family, as well as the numerous opportunities they've had to serve guests, they've been completely surrounded by those in the ministry. (Bob pastored Southeast Christian Church for forty years and now speaks all over the country, plus mentors young ministers at several retreats each year.)

Judy's going to show us how the table is a communal, bonding place:

Our table, where we gather for many meals, has been the key to growing all of our relationships. These mealtimes keep us in touch with each other, sealing our hearts and minds together, nurturing our souls.

Sweet fellowship happens around the table. Over the years, we've had a variety of guests (mostly in the ministry) who have put their feet under our table: family, friends, students, professors, authors, missionaries, preachers, political figures, coaches, sports figures, staff from church, college interns, Bible study groups, and neighbors.

When I was a child, the minister and his family would gather at our kitchen table and talk about working in foreign countries and other towns. We listened, laughed, cried, and prayed.

My mother used to make the most delicious meals, beginning with a beautifully prepared roast beef, flanked by a bounty of fresh steaming vegetables filling huge bowls. The grand finale was usually a homemade chocolate cake.

Our table wasn't fancy with china, crystal goblets, or real silver. But it was laden with the bounty God had provided. Bob's parents entertained many people at their table, as well. Naturally, it was easy for our family to follow suit.

There are seventy-six references in scripture about eating together at a table. Think about this for a moment: Our Lord, at birth, was laid in a feeding trough—a table for animals. And He broke bread with His disciples at His last meal, at a table!

> One tradition our family enjoys every Thanksgiving is when we pass the "Blessing Pot" at our table. Each person expresses something they are thankful for and shares why they're thankful.
>
> Prayer is also a vital part of every meal. These traditions as well as storytelling fill our hearts with love, comfort, and security, bringing laughter and joy to the table. If we really want to get to know someone's story, sitting down at the table and breaking bread together is the best way to start.

The Butter Babes have benefitted in many ways from sitting around Judy's table, usually for lunch. We know that when we sit down, we'll be there for a while. We savor the sacredness of our time, trust, and teaching around the table.

Judy also pulls off lovely dinners, even though she doesn't cook much anymore, save baking her infamous chocolate chip cookies for her grandchildren and other guests (she's my only friend who has a canister in her kitchen specifically for chocolate chips; you can bet I've partaken).

Judy also taught us her secret of entertaining: hunting and gathering. Tried and true dishes all around town can easily be ordered and picked up. We've now amassed quite the go-to list. One of our favorite go-tos is fetched from the Cheddar Box in Saint Matthews. The dish? Oh, sister-friend: the Hot Brown casserole.

The Hot Brown originated in Louisville at the Brown Hotel. Many a restaurant offers their own version, but I maintain the recipe at the end of this chapter (graciously given to us by the owner of the Cheddar Box) will make you the Pied Piper if you want to be. Trust me on this.

Author Shauna Niequist further expounds on her love for the table in her book, *Bread and Wine: A Love Letter to Life around the*

Table with Recipes. She suggests the table is a great leveler. At the end of the day, we all come with a need, finally slowing down enough to savor a meal and be ourselves.

I believe Shauna and Judy are encouraging us to grab a respite at the table. Everyone seated with us will bask in the beauty of sacred fellowship. Shauna adds, "If the home is the body, the table is the heart, the beating center, the sustainer of life and health."[6]

Faithful Friends Make the Best of Friends

Next up, I'd like for you to meet our fifth and final Butter Babe, Fay Bloyd. I was blessed to meet her while serving on a committee at church. We made an instant connection. My favorite story on Fay happened during our last move. My mother had passed away the same week we were to move into our current home. With relatives traveling from afar, we decided to go on and move, waiting a few days to have Mother's funeral.

Fay quickly organized a meal for after the funeral. How she coordinated all the people she did remains a mystery. The banquet table they prepared was the largest in our entertaining history. The men were like little boys that day, making multiple trips through the food line, the strength of their plates a huge gamble with the weight of their chosen entrees, sides, salads, rolls, and let's not forget dessert. Oh, the dessert.

My friend Meredith traveled from Nashville to come help us that weekend, plus to attend Mother's funeral. Our mothers were close friends, like Meredith and I are.

While we were all scurrying around, readying to go to the funeral, Meredith peeked out the window and saw several cars pull up. Multiple women hopped out, unloading casseroles, dishes, trays, pitchers, you name it.

Meredith announced, "The caterers are here."

I burst out laughing. "Nah, they're not caterers," I replied.

"They're my friends. They've come to put the meal together while we're at the funeral."

I suppose they *were* catering, but every single one of them are very dear to me, and I'll never forget what they did. Faithful Fay was at the helm, God bless her.

Blessed with a quiet spirit, Fay always makes me think of Romans 15:13: "May the God of hope fill you with all joy and peace as you trust in him, so that you may overflow with hope by the power of the Holy Spirit."

Another gift Fay has given us Babes is her gift of humor. One day, she picked me up while I was unable to drive, following foot surgery. I was getting around on an obnoxious scooter, aka Scott. Scott and I had an inseparable relationship, as he got me from point A to B quicker than crutches or a walker could.

Enter Fay to drive me to our beloved Teresa, our miracle worker, therapist, hair colorer, and stylist extraordinaire. Fay dropped me off, promising to pick me up to take me one more place we couldn't miss.

Game for another fun stop, Fay proceeded to pull up to a Hallmark store. In we went. (What an ordeal with Scott.) We literally hung out in the card section, creating quite a ruckus in the store. One card was funnier than another. It was the best therapy for my little feel-sorry-for-myself soul. Faithful Fay was also Funny Fay that day.

After all these years of friendship, Fay's decided being the baby of the Butter Babes has its advantages:

> Being the youngest of the Butter Babes, or the "Baby Babe," if you will, has provided me with amazing mentors over the past few years. These ladies have shared their godly wisdom, practical advice, parenting tips, and grandparenting prowess. They have shown how to care for aging parents, how to love and cherish your spouse, and how to be merciful caregivers when a loved one is sick.

Most importantly, they've modeled how to love people like Jesus would, how to connect people with effortless hospitality, and how to maintain a multitude of friendships while ensuring each one feels uniquely appreciated.

All of our schedules are incredibly full, but that makes the time we do have together all the sweeter. As a true Southern woman born and raised in the hills of eastern Kentucky, I know that even a dollop of butter makes anything, including my friendships, better.

Faithful friends bring peace, plus, as we've discussed this entire stop, faithful friends bring laughter and joy. The Butter Babes are not only faithful; they're as sweet as the tallest glass of sweet tea you could find. Yes, we are blessed.

Inspiration to Go

Sister-friend, keep on laughing, multiple times, every day. It's good for your health and extra good for your friends. And in the midst of laughter, you might just find that friendship doesn't have to be hard work. Gathering around the table will bond you and your friends together so easily, you won't realize it's happening. You can laugh and cry at the same time.

Consider these ways to meet new friends:
- Join a committee at your church (this is how I met Fay).
- Volunteer at your church or for a ministry in some capacity (this is how I met Judy).
- Go shopping (this is legit; this is how I met Nancy the Hugging Evangelist).
- Befriend a cousin (this is how I met Bonnie).
- Host a Christmas wrapping party. You and your friends will love it.

- Plan a long meal to give you and your friends a respite around a table.

As we move on down the road to our fifth stop, lace up your walkin' shoes. You're about to put a new kind of kick into your step.

Hot Brown Casserole-for-the-Soul
(From Nancy Tarrant, owner of the Cheddar
Box in St. Matthews, Louisville)

Before we dive in, you must know this dish is hands-down a favorite of everyone I know. I learned about it one day by accident after I blew into the Cheddar Box to pick up something for dinner. (Hunting and gathering are my primo talents, thanks to training from my friend, Judy, plus Fannie Flagg's mother's advice, which she reports has served her well: "Oh no, darling; you must *never* learn to cook or clean, or they will *expect* you to do to it."[7])

A gal in front of me was ordering a few servings of the Hot Brown casserole. I had no idea this was available, much less in any number of servings you'd like.

Well worth the experiment, I ordered two servings for John and me for dinner that night. Oh my, the sauce alone is so good, you can almost feel it clogging your arteries going down. This was a very bad discovery.

I'm now in the habit of ordering entire 9 × 13 casseroles to feed a crowd for dinner or lunch. The Butter Babes, in particular, are forever fans.

Nancy Tarrant, Cheddar Box's owner, and I are not only friends, we have a funny thing in common. She lives in a darling Cape Cod up the street from her store, which happens to be the very first home John and I lived in. We brought our first baby home there. There's just something special about your first home.

Nancy bought the house from the owner who bought it from us. One thing we realized, after the fact, was we'd forgotten to remove and replace a brass duck doorknocker (say that fast five times), which had been a wedding gift we'd hung on the front door.

It was too late to ask the owners for it, but once we learned years later that Nancy had bought it, John mentioned the doorknocker to her. Next thing we knew, she had it waiting for me the next time I stopped in her store. We now have it on the front door of John's man cave. So dear of Nancy.

Those of you living in Louisville know you can't go wrong with *any* dish you try from the Cheddar Box. It's the best go-to venue this cooking-impaired gal could have in her hunting and gathering arsenal.

Nancy makes all of us look good to our guests, which is a treasured gift. Read on, now, for a recipe your friends and family will beg for once you serve it:

Ingredients

For a 9 × 13 casserole:

2 pounds of roasted turkey, sliced thin

12 slices of bacon, fried and cut into small pieces

6 slices of toasted white bread (Nancy uses Pepperidge Farm bread)

Sliced tomatoes (enough to cover the top; maybe 2 or 3 whole tomatoes)

1½ cups grated cheddar cheese (she suggests aged New York cheddar, not Wisconsin)

Cheese Sauce (To die for, trust me)

¼ pound of butter

1 tablespoon chicken base paste (or chicken bouillon cube)

¼ cup flour

½ teaspoon salt

Pinch of black pepper

1½ quarts heavy cream

3 cups grated cheddar cheese

Directions

- Melt butter in a sauce pan over medium heat. Add flour and chicken base paste. Whisk until fully incorporated. Cook for about 5 minutes. Don't allow the butter to brown.

- Add cream and salt and pepper. Bring to a boil again over medium heat, stirring often. Once the mixture has come to a boil, remove from heat and gradually add the 3 cups of cheddar cheese. Allow to cool overnight.

To Assemble
- Place slices of toast into a 9 × 13 casserole dish.
- Layer turkey over the toast.
- Spread cheese sauce over the turkey.
- Top with sliced tomatoes.
- Sprinkle 1½ cups of cheddar cheese over the top of the tomatoes.
- Sprinkle bacon pieces over the top of the cheddar cheese.
- Bake at 350 degrees 30–45 minutes. Let rest for about 20 minutes before cutting.

Thank you, Nancy! We are forever indebted.

Fifth Stop: Soul-Stretching (Walking Buddies)

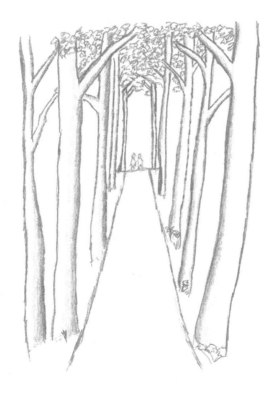

Those who walk with God always reach their destination.[1]
—Henry Ford

God is not only our Great Creator, He's our Great Connector. Watch this:

Connection #1: My friend Sherry gives me a newly released book, *Almost Amish—One Woman's Quest for a Slower, Simpler, More Sustainable Life* by Nancy Sleeth. We learned of this book because Sherry's daughter, Laura, Connection #2, was working for Nancy and her husband, Matthew, at the time.

Several of us read Nancy's book. (The Nancy in this chapter shall be called "Almost Amish Nancy," just to keep you from being confused. Who's on first, now?) We all unanimously love the book, want to meet Nancy, and invite her to come speak at our book club.

Invitation extended and accepted, five of us get to meet Almost Amish Nancy for dinner prior to her speaking at the book club. One of the five is Judy (yes, of the Butter Babes). Connection #3. The following year, Judy was to be the chair for the women's ministry portion of the North American Christian Convention (NACC).

Judy now extends an invitation to Nancy and Matthew to speak at the Minister's Wives Prayer Breakfast at the NACC. Connection #4. Matthew and Bob become friends and begin mentoring each other, while Judy and Nancy become forever friends, as well. Connection #5.

I'm beyond fortunate to declare Almost Amish Nancy as one of my dear friends and mentors. Connection #6. Plus, we mustn't forget it was Nancy who, after two years of watching their friendship bloom, encouraged Laura to finally accept a date with Stephen. By the way, Stephen and Laura wound up getting married. Now we have the perfect number, Connection #7. God abundantly blessed each of us when He created all of these connections.

Friendly Encounters

Nancy and I have logged many miles walking, trying to catch up from the last time we were together. When we meet up, we'll either walk and talk, or eat and talk, or both.

Do you see God's hand at work? This all happened so fast; if you told me I'd be blessed with a really smart, almost Amish friend, while I'm not nearly Amish, I'd have laughed my head off. Only God. We had the "What? You too?" conversation very early in our friendship.

The Sleeths live in Lexington, about seventy miles from Louisville. I'd walk to Lexington to partake of Nancy's homemade bread. Piping hot, with creamy butter melting down the side of her creation in *any* form is all the motivation I need. (She's gifted us, sister-friend, with one of her bread recipes on my website, and one of her chocolate desserts at the back of this chapter.)

Before you get to hear from Nancy, you must know she and Matthew take the Sabbath seriously. (Matthew wrote a moving book on the subject, *24/7: A Prescription for a Healthier, Happier Life*.) They're on a mission to cause the rest of us to do the same.

Here's one of my favorite quotes by Nancy. It's from an article she wrote for *Relevant Magazine*. She says, "Once a week, God walks out on the Sabbath Bridge to meet us. But most of us are no-shows; we unapologetically stand up the Creator of the universe, *week after week*."[2] I never thought about being a no-show, and it pains me to realize that's exactly what I've been on several Sabbaths.

I love learning new truths, however painful, from my friends. Friends like Nancy are what I call soul-stretching.

Nancy's also one of two friends who posed a tremendous uncomfortable yes to me about writing this book. More soul-stretching. She doesn't throw tiny projects your way; she likes ones that push you over on to the next, bigger, and much taller cliff's edge. Gulp.

As a matter of fact, all the women you'll meet in this chapter are soul-stretchers. They've shown me how to grow in a way that's uncomfortable at first, but in the end, indelible. You'll get to see what it looks like to nurture your soul and learn how walking is for talking; how to be ready to receive; why faith is not a solo sport; and how to invest in where you are.

In Their Own Words

As I think about my soul-stretching friends, it's true: We all do some sort of activity together, so we are active, as well. But I'm grateful I can count on these women to move me outside of my comfort zone. Their prodding equates to soul-stretching. In fact, Nancy asks a great question every time we're together: "How goes your soul?" Here's what she reveals about this key inquiry:

How Goes Your Soul?

Walking has become the single most important way I keep up with friends. We talk about kids, marriage, work, church, and aging parents—the stuff of everyday life—together. But it's more than that. We also ask, "How goes your soul?" We talk about what we are reading, what we hear God saying, and what we are learning. We ask for wisdom, from each other and from Jesus. And, always, we pray.

The best way I've found for deep conversations to happen is walking side by side, preferably outdoors. I've been walking with friends for three decades. I also walk with my husband, Matthew, my best friend, having made walking a thirty-six-year-long habit. Since becoming grandparents, many a morning, you'll find three generations of Sleeths walking together. I can't think of anything more beautiful.

I also walk to work most days. That's when I walk with my "bestest" friend, Jesus. These short walks alone with God are my chance to decompress, reflect, lift up problems, and pray for answers that seem impossible without Him. So often I've found myself dogged with a situation all day, and then, seemingly out of nowhere, on my walk to or from work, the answer appears. I just hadn't been walking close enough to Jesus to hear.

After our children finished college, we intentionally settled in a home where we could walk to everything—work, church, grocery store, hardware store, haircutter, pharmacy, dentist, library, restaurants, parks, theater; even the farmer's market is just a few blocks away. But I really hit the jackpot a couple years ago when three of my dearest friends (all from different cities) moved within walking distance of me. And now my grown kids, as well as their in-laws, all live within a few blocks. Life gets much simpler when the people and places you love are all in the neighborhood.

One of my friends recently asked me about my walking ministry. I had never thought of it that way. But I suppose ministry is about recognizing what is eternally important, and walking is how I focus on the things that matter most—my relationships with family, friends, and God—without distractions. So I guess I'll continue ministering to myself and my friends—and get a few miles in while I'm at it.

In addition to having a walking ministry, Nancy is a devoted prayer warrior. Whenever I email her about something, she always includes a personalized prayer just for me in her response. More often than not, I'll print it out because she's articulated my need better than I can, and I'll pray that to the Lord, telling Him, "This is what I really meant."

Additionally, I had never thought about Romans 12:2 within the walking realm prior to Nancy's thoughts: "Do not conform to the pattern of this world, but be transformed by the renewing of your mind." Walking friends help renew our minds. That's what I call soul-stretching.

Walking Is for Talking

Another walking buddy popped into my life as a complete surprise. My friend Lindsey and I were offering Pilates by the Pool, a summer program that included an hour of Pilates and an hour of Bible study. Before you hear of my lack of athleticism, let's just say Lindsey taught the Pilates, and I taught the Bible study.

We gathered around the pool deck, where Lindsey was about to teach Pilates. A tall, slender, swan-like woman opened the gate to come swim laps. Taken aback, she asked Lindsey what we were doing. Lindsey knew her and introduced us all to her friend, Mary Young. Mary was intrigued to learn of our summer program. We asked her to join us. She did so, and with great enthusiasm, joining us thereafter for every single class.

The rest, as they say, is history in that Mary and I became dear, dear friends from that day forward. We meet regularly to walk or to have lunch, never stopping long enough to take a breath, covering 101 topics. Mary's wisdom mirrors Proverbs 13:20 where it says, "Walk with the wise and become wise, for a companion of fools suffers harm."

We've begun a new habit of making lists of things to talk about for when we gather next. My cousin, Bonnie, taught me to do this, and it's become handier than ever, given the power of forgetfulness as we grow another year older. (That's tactful for saying we can't remember much more than our names these days.)

What I love about Mary is she walks with purpose. She builds friendship, enjoys nature, and exercises, all the while talking away:

> I love my friends, and I love walking. That winning combination is one of my favorite activities in life. When I walk with a friend, the stimulating conversation makes the walk seem like half the distance.

Sharing God's abundant gifts of nature with a friend, such as observing graceful deer, colorful singing birds, and lush trees, bushes, and flowers, is a spiritual experience. My heart soars in the fall when we behold a beautiful sunset with a backdrop of trees bursting with radiant hues as we make our way.

My friends and I discuss many subjects, sharing helpful information with one another. My husband travels a great deal, so I never feel lonely because of my walking companions. I am not a great multitasker, but I do gain a sense of accomplishment when we finish, knowing I'm closer to my friend and have also fulfilled my daily exercise goal.

My friends and I often meet at varied, scenic places, so on the drive home, I feel refreshed, empowered, and a bit wiser. We don't even have to be on a close fitness or skill level to enjoy walking together.

Some of my fondest memories in life are the hundreds of hours I've spent walking with my friends, or my husband, Michael, or my daughter, Lacy. I know without question I will be walking on a daily basis for as long as God allows.

I admire Mary's devotion to exercise. She rarely misses, whereas I can find an excuse to postpone my workout for pretty much any reason. Walking with a friend gets you out there moving, whether you want to or not. I tend to side with actress Caroline Rhea, who said, "My favorite machine at the gym is the vending machine. "[3]

What a ginormous relief to know one doesn't have to be athletic to be a friend. If that were the case, I'd be disqualified lickety-split.

My PE teacher in elementary school had the gall to inform my mother I couldn't hit the broad side of a barn with a softball. Super proud of that.

Daddy wanted me to be a tennis player. He thought having his little girl become his newfound tennis buddy would be quite the bee's knees. He and Mother sacrificed big bucks to send me to tennis camp.

I came home with a trophy.

For gymnastics.

Once out of college, I landed my first real job, and my office had a softball team (should've been a clue). After a coworker extended an invitation to join them, I blurted out, "Yes! I'd love to."

Being sports illiterate, I found out the hard way you can run through first base; you don't have to stop on a dime on the base. "Out!" the umpire hollered. Coach had to give me quick Cliff's Notes on the game of softball while my coworker was visibly regretting his invitation.

Ready to Receive

Our Lord continues to have a sense of humor to connect me with my dear friend, Sherry Leavell. We missed each other by a few years at UK because she was ahead of me, in more ways than one (all good, I might add).

I didn't know until recently Sherry was a lettered athlete, having played on the UK golf team. This is a huge feat. To this day, she and her husband, Bill, are megatalented golfers, with single-digit handicaps.

Sherry's a real-live jock but thankfully isn't on an ego trip about it. Our paths crossed through mutual friends, ultimately landing us in the book club. This was how we began our soul-stretching together.

In addition to learning more about God through books in the book club, Sherry and I often took the same Bible study, either together or in different groups, and we'd share what we were learning. I'd love to tell you we log many miles walking together, but to be honest, we probably spend more time eating salmon salad or creating something fun to eat with our spiralizers (she left me in the dust with that little contraption).

One of many favorite things I love about Sherry is she's sincerely intentional about her faith. One dead-of-winter January day, an email from Sherry popped up. She'd written twelve friends, asking, "Anyone free to meet for lunch at Brasserie Provence today? Noon?"

Amazingly, eight of the twelve of us were free. Off we plowed through the snow, ready for one of the best quiches in town (oh, the buttery crust makes my mouth water).

A few introductions were necessary, as a couple of us didn't know each other. We all agreed that any friend of Sherry's is a friend to know.

Sherry began by saying, "You'll see you each have two cards. Choose one and let us learn more about you." We learned pretty quick these little cards pack a punch. On one side, there's a question, and on the other, a scripture. I could feel an uncomfortable yes comin' on, thinking I had no brilliant answer to offer. That was obviously the father of lies messin' with me. Thankfully, we had two options, and I bravely chose the easier of the two. Deep. More soul-stretching.

Check out some of these excellent questions and try them the next time you have a gathering of your friends:

> What is one thing in your life you tend to take for granted? (This one had Psalm 107:8 on the back: "Let them give thanks to the Lord for His unfailing love and his wonderful deeds for mankind.")
>
> What do you hope to pass on to the next generation?
>
> What is one of your favorite characteristics of God? Why?
>
> Who has encouraged you lately? What did they say?
>
> How has God shown you His grace?

We called one another to action by adding two very scary words to the end of the questions: "this week," producing immediate action, application, and accountability. While savoring hot French bread with olive oil, cracked pepper, and sea salt (as if one could possibly think with such heavenly offerings), one by one, we began to learn more about each other and about where God was working. Awestruck, I came away encouraged to see the hand of God in so many lives.

I'm so thankful our calendars were open that day. From that impromptu lunch, we each took home a warm blessing on a cold winter's day. That's what soul-stretching friends do. Watch now how Sherry shows us her friends as an example of Proverbs 27:17, about iron sharpening iron:

Faith Is Not a Solo Sport

The Lord often uses *people* to bring us to Himself and to grow us in our faith. We have His Word and the Holy Spirit, but we also have the gift of other believers to help us grow. How about you? Have you also found that that faith is not a solo sport?

Many of these *people* have been men: preachers, teachers, my husband, my pastor son-in-law, and others.

But it's really *my girlfriends* that have taught me the most about walking with the Lord. There is something about women and Bible study, where laughter, tears, confession, and transparent sharing occurs that really grows and stretches us as women.

My mentor, Tatter, gave me the precious gift of being able to pray with others. She would say to me, "Let's just pray about that" (whatever it was), and then, "Would you like to pray first or second?" I would usually say second and would listen to her pray and then would open my mouth and pray. The more I prayed with Tatter, the easier it became, and I found myself saying the same thing to others: "Let's pray. Do you want to go first or second?"

My closest and favorite friends are the ones who share "God stories" with me. These are the gals who would rather talk about God than about others. They help me see Him in every area of my life. There have been countless times when I may have overlooked a hidden blessing had it not been for friends. They regularly share prayer requests and also God's answers to prayers. They keep me excited about the Lord and my relationship with Him.

My girlfriends and I memorize scripture, share Christian books, serve others, pray, and study. They weep with me when I am struggling and rejoice with me when all is well (Romans 12:15).

Paul David Tripp says, "God's care comes in many forms. Fellowship is God caring enough to put people in your life to encourage, rebuke, and comfort you."[4]

What a wonderful purpose and plan. It sure makes our journeys of faith much more fun than flying solo.

I loved discovering more about Proverbs 17:17 after reading Sherry's words; they jumped off the page in one of the many books Liz Curtis Higgs has written, which now ranks as one of my favorites: *31 Verses to Write on Your Heart*. One of the thirty-one verses is our iron sharpening iron one. She says, "This verse is short, sweet, and ... um, sharp.... The Hebrew word *rea* means not just any person but a 'friend, companion, fellow, neighbor.' Someone we know well. Someone we care about and who cares about us."[5] Just like my soul-stretching friends here in this chapter.

Liz gives us a fun visual: "The Hebrew word *paneh* means 'face.' Literally, 'friends sharpen each other's faces.'"[6] Don't you love that? As God grows us to be more like Him, let's be intentional to sharpen each other's faces. (The store Sharper Image has just taken on a whole new meaning. Smile.)

Invest Where You Are

I mentioned Sherry's daughter, Laura, earlier. She was Connection #2 at the beginning of this stop. She's another old soul, now livin' in the South, in Alabama. I'm not the only one who misses her. Her family does, obviously, and Almost Amish Nancy does because Laura kept Nancy and Matthew's nonprofit, Blessed Earth, running like a top. It was really quite sacrificial of Nancy to actively support the budding Laura-Stephen courtship, knowing they'd be leaving if it led to marriage.

John and I were blessed to attend Laura and Stephen's wedding. I found it intriguing when their minister spoke of the importance of the table, citing the same concept Judy tells us about around her table. Hospitality is definitely one of Laura's and Stephen's gifts, which goes hand in hand beautifully when you're in ministry.

While her transition from Lexington to Tanner, Alabama, has been challenging, I love what she so willingly has taught me about change. Friendships can survive long distance, and new ones thankfully pop up. Watch Laura's transform after her recent move:

> When discussing friendship, it's easy to wax poetic about lifelong friendships, high school pals that remain close, and neighbors that never move away. Many of us never consider we might need to start from scratch and develop new friendships multiple times throughout our lives.

I recently confronted this reality when I married my husband, Stephen, a Methodist pastor who is assigned to his ministry job by the denominational leadership.

We had to transition to north Alabama.

In Kentucky, I had a great setup for friendships. I'd been involved in my church for over five years, many of my closest friends served in ministry with me there, several of my family members lived in town, and the rest were just an hour away.

When I moved to Alabama, all of that changed. While I was happy to be in the same place as Stephen, I struggled. I yearned for my friends in Kentucky and the many networks I'd developed. I missed going to church with people that were so much like me.

Many days I felt like I hated Alabama and wanted to move back to Kentucky. I was reluctant to embrace the people in my new home because I felt like I was betraying those I had left behind in my old home.

Now, many months later, my friendship situation is a lot better. There are three main lessons I've learned through this:

First, invest in where you are. For example, my husband just became the pastor of a rural church, Tanner United Methodist Church. Our house and church back up to a K–12 school, so we attend all the home football games and cheer for the Tanner Rattlers, while wearing green Rattlers shirts.

After the games, we open up the church gym for our 5th Quarter Outreach with the youth and their families. Was this something I pictured myself doing in Kentucky? No, but it's been a great way to meet our neighbors in our new community. I've found this adage to be true: the grass isn't necessarily greener in another place; the grass is greener where you water it.[7]

Second, be open to making friends with people who are different from you. Some of my friendships in Alabama have been very different from those in Kentucky. My first close friend in Alabama was a mom with three children. Although I'm not a parent, we have connected over our faith and love of walking and running.

Another friend is much older than I am, but we laugh about our pets and discuss current events. Two of my favorite colleagues are not believers, but we connect in many other ways. Many of these friends are quite different from those friends in Kentucky, and I've been surprised by how I've enjoyed expanding my friendship circle.

Third, try to be content in seasons when you don't have many friends, knowing the season will likely pass. This has been a tough realization, but it's an important one. In this season, my husband has had to become my best friend because he is my primary friend here.

Back in Kentucky, I had social engagements many nights of the week. In Alabama, I've had many more nights coming straight home after work, and many weekend nights staying in with my husband.

For a doer who likes to make things happen, it's difficult to realize it's okay if there are seasons where you lack a variety of friends but can focus on your marriage. If you're single, it can be valuable to have seasons of loneliness where you focus on growing in your faith or learning more about yourself.

> Starting over socially is never easy and rarely preferable, but it can be a great opportunity for growing your faith, yourself, and your heart for others.

What season do you find yourself in right now? Dare I divulge I'm in a season of contentment? I've been through a few winter seasons, and I know they'll blow in again. But thanks to Laura and her soul-stretching wisdom, I pray I'll be ready to receive as she has done.

I'll close this stop with who I now call South Carolina Sue. We were once neighbors, but sadly, she and her husband, Randy, moved away from Louisville. They're currently living in Bluffton, South Carolina, thence her moniker.

When we were neighbors, she and Randy would pique our curiosity every winter. They'd don coats, hats, scarves, and mittens, and walk their dog, Yogi, down snow-covered streets. They were always armed with a steaming cup of coffee. They moved from Toledo, Ohio, where they learned the outdoors is always available; one just must dress the part. (I observed all this while clad in flannel pajamas with my steaming cup of coffee from inside our home.)

Sue and I walked together too. Before they moved to South Carolina, they lived in Michigan. One summer, John and I went up to visit them. They lived on Lake Michigan near Petoskey, in a gorgeous area called Bay Harbor. Sue and I left our boys (as in husbands) splashing in Lake Michigan, opting to take Yogi for a walk. One of many things we share together, in addition to walking, is our love for looking at homes. Some of those homes on the lake are take-your-breath-away stunning.

Sue recently sent me a never-so-true quote from Doe Zantamata: "Good friends help you to find important things when you have lost them. Your smile, your hope, and your courage."[8] Just like the booster shot I talked about with the Butter Babes. Sue also added a PS: "Oh and good friends always know when a yummy piece of chocolate is needed!" To which I shout a resounding Amen, being the consummate chocoholic I am. Furthermore, may we count steps, not calories (Bigger smile).

Inspiration to Go

Walking and talking with your friends empowers you to

- grow your soul (ask, "How goes your soul?"),
- be ready to receive,
- look for ways to sharpen each other,
- invest where you are,
- be more intentional,
- walk with Jesus, and
- experience time management at its finest by catching up and walking with your friends. Cheerfully cross "exercise" off your list for the day, while also stretching your soul.

Check with your church or neighborhood about a walking group, or maybe start one yourself. Our daughter-in-love, LT, is in a walking group she and several friends started who live in adjacent neighborhoods. They walk for an hour every Monday night.

As we stretch before a workout, may we be soul-stretching sister-friends, encouraging each other to take the next necessary step.

Let's move on to our next stop where you'll get to meet a unique trio of women. 'Tis time for tea, scones, and other sweet treats to uncover.

Chocolate Nemesis (Gluten-Free)
(also from Nancy Sleeth)

One delightful discovery in my friendship with Almost Amish Nancy is we both love chocolate. A superb "What? You too?"

It's a bonus for all of us because not only is this recipe crazy good, it's gluten free and loaded with chocolate.

Ingredients
½ cup of water
¾ cup of sugar
6 oz. of unsweetened chocolate (chopped)
3 oz. of semi-sweet chocolate (chopped)
¾ cup (1½ sticks) of butter, sliced
3 large eggs

Toppings
Frozen strawberries with sugar (defrosted)
8 oz. of heavy cream whipped with 3 tablespoons of sugar until stiff
1 oz. of semi-sweet chocolate (shaved)

Directions
- Butter a 10-inch springform pan and line with wax paper.
- Preheat oven to 350 degrees.
- In medium saucepan, bring water to a boil and stir in sugar until dissolved. Turn down the heat to lowest setting and stir in chocolate and butter until melted. Remove from heat and cool slightly before whisking in eggs.
- Pour chocolate into springform pan. Place springform in a larger pan. Fill larger pan with ½ inch of water and bake for 30 minutes until the middle is set.

- Refrigerate until firm before serving. Top each slice with defrosted strawberry slices with some juice, a dollop of fresh whipped cream, and the semi-sweet chocolate shavings.

Yum!

Sixth Stop: Mentoring
(Friends from Tea)

He that is thy friend indeed,
He will help thee in thy need,
If thou sorrow he will weep,
If thou wake he cannot sleep.
—William Shakespeare

"Wherefore art thou, Romeo?"
    Nope.
    "To be or not to be, that is the question."
    Nope.
    "To sip tea and partake of warm scones with butter."

Yes, *that* is the answer.

Oh, and you must be named Elizabeth.

Strict, and I mean strict rules apply to this mahhhvelous trio. (Hey, if you're named Elizabeth, mosey on over.)

Meet the Elizabethan Sisters. We're quite the threesome: one in our fifties, one in our sixties, and one in our seventies. Elizabeth Jeffries, Liz Curtis Higgs, and I have been dear friends for years.

The three of us simply began meeting one day for lunch. We initially met through mutual friends, hitting it off instantly, three for three resounding "What? You too?" We decided we'd heretofore be known as the Elizabethan Sisters. (Oh, the name game.) Our mantra is a picture of Romans 14:19 that says, "Let us therefore make every effort to do what leads to peace and to mutual edification." Yes, there's edification *and* education every time I'm with these sweet sister-friends.

Friendly Encounters

Text messages and emails fly back and forth between the Elizabethan Sisters on a regular basis. We all live in Louisville, yet my Elizabethan Sisters are found hopping planes like you and I hop into a car. Thus, it takes hugely intentional calendar coordinating to get us together tête-à-tête. Further challenging, one of us happens to be a renowned author who's perpetually under a book deadline. (Can you guess?)

"Elizabethan" sounds as if tea could be involved. That's a given at each gathering whether we're at a lovely, quiet, linen-covered table in a froo-froo restaurant or plopped down at a wood-n-metal table in a noisy Starbucks.

When we do escape to see one another, we're usually celebrating the completion of a book by Liz. One time, I gave her an oversized pair of sunglasses to wear, since she hadn't left her house for weeks. I warned her she'd be blinded by the daylight. That was the year she was writing *Here Burns My Candle.* Trust me, she soooo burned a lot of candles at both ends to finish that one.

Other times, we celebrate Christmas or each other's birthdays. My time with these gals is a double blessing because they're not only friends, they're mentors armed with a wealth of information and life experiences. Regardless of what we're going through, grace covers our conversation. Thankfully judgment is non-existent. That's what mentoring friends do.

The Elizabethan Sisters have been creating memories for years, but a favorite one happened at Corbett's Restaurant in Louisville (now sadly closed). It was in a lovely old Cape Cod, complete with beautiful décor and the best sweet potato fries one could wish for, not that one needed a motivation to dine there.

After ordering iced tea, we were presented with a bread basket of several different types of rolls, each one a vision. Hunks of butter at the ready, we happily placed our orders and settled in to catch up with each other.

Suddenly, Liz whipped out two copies of her soon-to-be-released novel. We'd been praying her through the writing process, while anxiously awaiting this baby. (As of this writing, she's now birthed thirty-seven books.) This novel happened to be a sequel, which made the waiting that much more painful for us impatient folk.

Something was up with Liz. She was like a still-believes-in-Santa-Claus kid. "Open it!" she squealed.

Elizabeth and I opened the book. There were our names. Liz dedicated *Mine Is the Night* to us. We all three had tears rolling down our faces. I can't say I can recall such a unique gift. Ever.

We remained speechless, but not for long. More words flowed over our hot soups and salads than our poor waiter could comprehend. As usual, we nearly closed the restaurant down. We hightailed it home to, of course, dive into our new novels.

One shared trait I love about my Elizabethan Sisters is they are devoted disciples of our Lord. They have another group of friends that meets annually for a retreat. It's not just to catch up and shop. One of the women plans several teaching times, with the main objective being to learn more from the Word of God.

Knowing my Elizabethan Sisters and by extension these new friends, I can tell you their desire to learn is infectious. They all glow with the light of Christ, spreading their sparkle everywhere. I'm not kidding. (Hey, my new blush has sparklies in it; does that count? Pitiful... I know.)

In Their Own Words

I like to call my Elizabethan Sisters and the Birthday Bunch (who you'll soon meet) mentoring friends. They've shown me what it means to be beloved, determined, a learned traveler, and a vivacious celebrator.

A Favorite Word

As you've probably already figured out, Liz Curtis Higgs plays a prominent role in my life. The cool thing about knowing a talented and gifted author is, your friendship becomes a double blessing: You learn from her writing, and you get to learn from her one-on-one.

Liz uses a favorite-to-me word not only in her writing, but also when we talk. It makes me dissolve into a tearful puddle. She's still teaching me what it means to be this word, because that's what mentoring friends do. You'll get to hear it very soon.

When our mutual friend, Naomi, came to speak at our church's Christmas tea, I threw together a brunch for her and her daughter, inviting lots of girls from our Bible studies, and Liz. You've never heard such chattering with all those women.

This was the first time Liz had been to our home. It had a very cool fifteen- by thirty-foot entry hall, which always took visitors by surprise. She walked in and came to a complete halt. "Oh dear," she sighed.

Oh, no, I thought. *What could be wrong?*

To which she replied in half a second, "I need to lower my covet meter."

We all cracked up. Classic.

Not too long after that, Liz invited me to attend a Women of Faith event in Columbus, Ohio. A road trip with Liz? Are you kidding me? We were long on talk, filled to overflowing from the Women of Faith gals, and short on sleep. But oh-so-happy.

On our trip back to Louisville, Liz posed an interesting opportunity. This was my first uncomfortable yes with her.

She said, "You know, you really ought to start writing a blog. It's a good discipline and would prepare you to write a book."

This was impeccable timing on Liz's part, as we had three-plus hours to lay out such a thought. Five plus years and another uncomfortable yes later, you know how that's transpired because here I sit, writing this book.

Liz was also my first friend to literally pray over me. When we lived near each other, she called one morning and said, "Hey, I had you on my mind. What's up?"

I nearly dropped the phone because our little family was going through a bit of a crisis. She had no idea, but God did.

She said, "Want to come over?"

I was there in three minutes.

She said, "Let's pray about this." And she stood over me, put her hands on my shoulders, and prayed grace-filled words heavenward to our Sovereign God, renewing my hope and faith. I'll never forget it.

Finally, I must share one little word with (and for) you, sister-friend. As I alluded to earlier, Liz uses a certain word that sends me reeling every time she uses it.

After I relayed my reaction to this word, Liz gifted me with a plaque that now hangs in my office. It says, "Beloved, God chose you from the beginning." This comes from 2 Thessalonians 2:13, which says, "But we ought always to thank God for you, brothers and sisters loved by the Lord, because God chose you as firstfruits to be saved through the sanctifying work of the Spirit and through belief in the truth."

The word? "Beloved," of course. Liz uses this beautiful,

mind-blowing word in all of her books, in her talks, and with her friends. Just like being on the receiving end of grace is tough to grasp for some of us, ditto for being God's beloved, His chosen. Oh, but it's so true. All praise goes to you, Lord.

I think Liz says it best when she talks about how God shows us we are indeed beloved:

When I was diagnosed with endometrial cancer, you *know* my Elizabethan sisters rallied around, despite my insisting, "I'm fine! Don't need a thing!"

Elizabeth Jeffries slipped into my darkened hospital room early one morning, bearing an extra-hot venti chai latte from Starbucks. When she found me tucked beneath the covers, she quietly put the tea where I could find it and whispered, "You're in good hands, Liz. The Holy Spirit is all around you." Even as she spoke those words, He affirmed His presence with His peace. Oh, glory.

And when I came home from the hospital to find our fridge empty, Elizabeth Hoagland texted me describing a mouthwatering dinner she was making for her family. "Be right over!" I texted back in jest. The next day, she appeared at our door with all the scrumptious leftovers, from salad to dessert. Who does that? A friend who won't take no for an answer.

Sometimes, when we think God isn't near or doesn't care, we can look at those who *are* near and *do* care, and realize they are God's hands and feet, delivering tangible proof of His love.

Like the day another friend, Fifi, came over to rub my feet, which were aching from chemo-induced neuropathy (it's a thing). It was humbling for me to say, "Sure, come on over and massage my feet." But I did, and she did, and it was holy and sacred and beautiful. Yes, they were Fifi's hands, but it was God's touch. This is how He shows up. This is how He ministers to our needs.

And the nurse and hospital secretary who appeared in my little pre-op cubicle just before surgery? I knew they were believers and asked if they would pray for me, thinking they'd do so on their own. You know, maybe later. Nope. They pulled the curtain shut and prayed right then. Tenderly. Fearlessly. Who does that? Two women who love Jesus.

Sometimes, God sends us friends we've known for ages. And sometimes, He brings us new friends to assure us we are beloved.

May we all savor the word *beloved* and believe it is true about ourselves, thanks to Liz's dear words and the Word of God. Amen and amen.

Determined

Well, let's meet the other sister of our Elizabethan Sisters, Elizabeth Jeffries. She can accomplish more than a dozen of my friends can in half the time. Where she gets her energy is beyond me.

Elizabeth's my most determined friend. One year, the year of a milestone birthday, she determined she was going to spend ninety days in Florence, Italy. Can you imagine? One of her many motives is she's Italian and wanted to learn more firsthand about her heritage, submerging herself into the culture.

It just so happened John and I were going on a trip to Italy that wound up in Florence while she'd be there. Long before she and her husband, Stephen, left, she called me with the invitation to beat all invitations: "Would you and John like to spend a few extra nights with me? I'll still be in Florence when you get there."

About half a second later, I blurted out, "Yes! Yes! Yes!"

Our three days and nights with Elizabeth are still some of our fondest memories of our Italian adventure. By the time we arrived at her place, she had the streets and city figured out. Every day we marched to the nearby market and chose fresh vegetables, pasta, and sauces to conjure up something remarkable for lunch. *Buon appetito*! Determined, I'll say.

Every night, we tried a different restaurant, each one more delicious than the night before. The freshest of ingredients coupled with insanely talented chefs made for heaven on earth. Technically, John and I aren't of Italian heritage, just desperate wannabes. We could eat pasta three meals a day. Makes my mouth water just to talk about. We praise you, Lord.

John and I are forever grateful for Elizabeth's determination to plan such a trip. We'll never forget the many memories we made, all the while getting to be mentored by Elizabeth. Let's listen in now as she so eloquently defines friendship for us:

> The word *sister* literally means "having parents in common." Technically, since Adam and Eve are the parents of all of us, it seems pretty logical all my friends are my sisters!
>
> You can have acquaintances, colleagues, and friends, but sisters, well, that's a cookie of a different flavor! I'm definitely related, connected, and bound to, as well as loved by each of these women. We laugh with each other, tease each other, forgive each other, sing over each other, do high tea together, and, well, eat pretty much anything together, especially chocolate.

Sometimes our eyes leak when we're sharing something painful, but a Sister is always ready with Kleenex. We hold each other up, keep each other from jumping over the cliff, and speak the truth in love when it's needed.

Sisters come to your speeches and your one-woman show and start the standing ovation at the end. Not because *you* are great, but because *they* are. Sisters bring you food when you're sick, flowers when you celebrate, books they love and can't wait to share, fun gifts they just happen to see and know you'd love, and fly swatters when they know you need to chase Satan out of your home.

The tie that binds us, though, is Jesus. We pray for and with each other, whether it's as serious as a surgery or as earth-shattering as needing a new manicurist. We pray for each other's marriages, children, work, travels, and homes; lately, many prayers are for health.

"Just Call My Name," "I'll Stand by You," or "You've Got a Friend." However you sing it, if you have even one sister, you are blessed indeed! And I thank my God every time I think of her.

Elizabeth and I have a new prayer assignment now that she's mentioning prayers for her sister-friends for health. The warrior in us has surfaced, and we are sportin' red boxing glove emojis in every text we share with Liz.

I cannot believe Liz has cancer. This is another huge uncomfortable yes we've uttered, but we Elizabethan Sisters won't leave each other's side, wherever we may be in this world. We'd appreciate it if you'd stop for a moment and pray for our Lizzie. As Elizabeth said, that's what sister-friends do.

Traveling Homework

While Elizabeth and Liz travel the world speaking, traveling with other couples can be fantastic too. Thanks to my Elizabethan Sisters and the book club, we are blessed with a mutual friend, Carol Bonura. Carol and her husband, Joe, helped form a sixsome that travels and learns together. Elizabeth and Stephen, along with Jim and Naomi Rhode, complete their group. They call each other the Souljourners, which I was elated to learn about, especially with such a fun name. They've been traveling together for almost two decades.

More importantly, I learned this group has a faith purpose, as well. I quickly discovered they're mentoring friends just by virtue of what they do when they leave town. They look for ways to grow their faith along the way.

One New Year's Eve, we were all over at Elizabeth and Stephen's. True to Elizabeth's form, she posed a question about what were some of our favorite things we did in the past year. Carol's reply caused me to nearly fall out of my chair when she revealed she'd read sixty-five books that year. Impressive.

Watch how she has fun learning something new while traveling with the Souljourners:

> When we find friends who encourage us, inspire us, and make us want to be *better* than we are, then those friendships are the ones we want to encourage and cherish because they're a rarity.
>
> My Souljourners define this type of friendship. We have a common denominator of faith, so we also inject that element into our travels. Each time we travel, Naomi assigns us a book or project, and we present our findings in the morning during our devotional time.

Carol's Souljourners have traveled the world. They learn from and mentor each other while learning about wherever their travels have led them. The details of their trips read like a fabulous travelogue. (You can find them on my website, www.elizabethhoagland.com, under Contributor's Essays. Search for Carol Bonura.)

Don't Forget to Celebrate

I'm throwing in another group of gals to share with you whose mission is super simple. You and your friends can effortlessly copy this idea: Gather for a meal once a month and celebrate a birthday. This couldn't be any easier. We're up to about sixteen chickies, so we usually have at least one birthday girl each month, sometimes several. I actually crashed the group several years ago.

The name? Depends on who you ask. We're known as the Birthday Bunch as well as Birthday Girlfriends. All that matters is who's having a birthday. The birthday girl becomes our focus. We show up and bring a rather irreverent card for her. One gal who moved away used to be the best card finder, and in the most spiritual of ways, she'd always sign it, "In Christ." Forgive us, Lord.

Another interesting aspect of this group is all of us are in different Bible studies. This makes for fascinating conversation. We've been known to trade DVDs back and forth too. Double blessing.

The other realization (now a triple blessing) is we all wind up mentoring each other from sharing about our various Bible studies, some of us teaching helpful aspects from these studies. Added hints on what works and what doesn't saves time and sweat equity for us when we lead our other groups.

My dear friend, Ginny Crowe, was part of this Birthday Bunch. Her husband had the nerve to accept a job in Indianapolis. They recently moved, and we miss her terribly. She popped in for one of our birthday get-togethers last summer.

That's when I begged Ginny to explain the Birthday Bunch for you:

There are two rules for Birthday Bunch: #1. You have to have a birthday, and #2. You must bring an impolite yet funny card for the birthday girl. Most people struggle with rule #2 when they first join. The idea of bringing a rude card to a lovely Christian woman seems wrong. But if you bring a sappy, "Jesus loves you, and so do I," sentiment, you will be mocked. New members quickly catch on to rule #2!

I'll never forget receiving my first set of birthday cards from the club. They were just awful! I put the stack in my car and drove straight from lunch to carpool. My middle school-aged son picked up the cards to read them, and I let out a scream and yelled, "Stop!" There were things he *might* have understood, but if he didn't, I sure didn't want to be the one doing the explaining. I took the cards home, pushed them down in the trashcan, and covered them with more trash. The birthday girls are serious about rule #2.

Each Birthday Girl is special to me. That happens when you meet once a month for over ten years, sharing life in a way that bonds us together in Christian love and fellowship. The group assembles, and it's different each time. Sometimes we hug, sometimes we laugh, cry, or do all of the above. But it's rule #2 that ensures we always scream (those birthday cards). We've had many occasions of laughing so hysterically over those terrible cards that the entire restaurant stares. I've overheard servers tell other tables, "They're only drinking Diet Coke!"

I don't want to leave you with the impression that we only laugh and have superficial fun. We can be serious. It happens each month when we encounter the normal struggles of life--the things common to all who live in this broken world. Pain has touched each of us, just as it has pierced your life. And yet, it is good to have friends who encourage, care, and laugh with you through your trials and victories.

Psalm 126:2 perfectly depicts the Birthday Bunch: "Our mouths were filled with laughter, our tongues with songs of joy. Then it was said among the nations, 'The Lord has done great things for them.'"

There is laughter *and* shouting, and while it might not be said among the nations, it's certainly noticed by other restaurant patrons that the Lord has done great things for us, because we have laughter, joy, and friendships. Rule #2 guarantees it!

(Hint: Our author, Elizabeth, has an August birthday. She likes dark chocolate, and if you can combine that with rule #2, then you've got a winning card to send her!)

Yes, well, I was going to edit out that little hint from Ginny, but I just couldn't. You must also know I consider Ginny another genius friend. She has written two excellent Bible studies, one on Joshua and the other on Hebrews.

Believe it or not, the Birthday Bunch now meets at night, and several of us, myself included, are no longer able to attend. Schedules have gotten crazy. But while the season lasted, each birthday gal was blessed, encouraged, and mentored in the most special of ways.

Inspiration to Go

Like all of these friends from all of these stops, this is another case for laughter being the best medicine.

The other takeaways come from my Elizabethan Sisters. Let's embrace the concept of mentoring, beloved. Lovely smile. You can tell the Elizabethan Sisters and the Birthday Bunch major in mentoring.

While the idea of traveling with your friends is obviously exciting, my two Elizabethan Sisters are traveling experts, therefore teaching me great places to go and things to do. Who knew mentoring would include travel tips? How fun is that?

And while we're at it, who knew determination could be a mentoring tool? I determined from our Italy trip I frequently need a dose of determination from Elizabeth Jeffries and pray I can pass it on in some helpful form to someone else. My trips with these gals go down in our friendship history as blissful treasures.

Like Liz, be all in.

Like Elizabeth Jeffries, be intentional with your calendar.

Like both of them, look around you for people to mentor. Do not say (like I have in the past), "I don't have anything to offer." Yes, you do. Just make the phone call, meet for coffee or lunch, or go for a walk. The Lord will bless your efforts.

Try some fun, educational travel with your friends, like Carol does with her Souljourners. As we age, not only does our body need physical exercise, our brains need mental exercise. What better way than with friends to learn something new?

Start a birthday group. Celebrate birthdays, and uncover ways to mentor each other. You'll have a win-win on your hands.

Brace yourself, we're about to dive in to some heavy-duty subject matter. I suggest you go brew a hefty cup of coffee or tea, as you'll need to be uber alert for the next stop.

Spinach Salad with Honey Vinaigrette from the Bluebird Café in Stanford, Kentucky
(from Chef Bill Hawkins)

Another road trip the Butter Babes took after their escapades at the Castle was a lovely drive to Stanford, Kentucky. A writer friend we'd only met via email, Angela Correll, invited us to have lunch at her restaurant, the Bluebird Café.

Once inside the restaurant, Angela motioned for us to sit down. She and Fay locked eyes, simultaneously saying, "Didn't you go to Georgetown College?"

Our six degrees of separation diminished that day while our waistlines expanded, thanks to the delicious food we inhaled at the Bluebird. Angela and the Butter Babes had many "What? You too?" conversations. We immediately declared her to be an ancillary member.

Not only did we have a fabulous time together talking, eating, and of course, laughing, we also enjoyed shopping in Angela's store across the street from the restaurant, Kentucky Soaps and Such, taking home several treasures, including her amazing goat's milk body cream.

Her chef has graciously offered us the recipe for his delicious spinach salad:

Ingredients

Honey Vinaigrette
1 tablespoon Dijon mustard
¼ cup apple cider vinegar
3 tablespoon local honey
¾ cup olive oil
Salt and pepper to taste

Vanilla Almonds

½ teaspoon vanilla extract

2 oz. slivered almonds

Salad Ingredients

3 oz. spinach

2 oz. goat cheese

2 oz. strawberries

Directions

- Sautee the almonds and vanilla extract on medium high heat until toasted golden. Pour onto another surface and spread out to cool.
- Mix the Dijon mustard, honey, and apple cider vinegar together. While continuing to whisk those ingredients, add in the olive oil slowly until emulsified. Add salt and pepper to taste. Set aside.
- Rinse and slice the strawberries. Rinse the spinach and put in a bowl. Gently toss the strawberries, spinach, and desired amount of honey vinaigrette. Top with goat cheese and almonds.
- Amounts shown for salad ingredients are individual portions, so multiply as needed.

One of Joe Daniels's Many Favorite Italian Dishes
Homemade Meatballs and Spaghetti Sauce
(from Kathy Hampton Daniels and her son, Matt,
affectionately known to us as Matt D.)

I referenced Joe's Italian heritage on our second stop, where you met the Ya-Yas. Since I talk about the Ya-Yas being "meatball friends" (see Bible study questions), it seemed natural to use Carm's meatball recipe (Carm was Joe's mother). Kathy made this recipe countless times for countless hungry souls, the Yas-n-Yos many time the beneficiaries.

Ingredients
1½ pound of ground sirloin
⅔ cup bread crumbs
⅔ cup grated Pecorino Romano cheese
1 serving spoon of pepper
1 serving spoon of salt
1 clove of garlic, finely chopped
7 eggs

Directions
- Place sirloin in a large mixing bowl. Cover with bread crumbs. Add grated Pecorino Romano cheese. Cover with a serving spoon of pepper and then a serving spoon of salt. Add chopped garlic and eggs. Mix all of this well with your hands.
- Fry in lard at medium to high heat. Do not burn. Turn meatballs occasionally with a fork. Change grease in the pan if it starts to burn or brown. After frying the meatballs, add them to the tomato sauce.

Gram's Sauce

While Kathy could make this sauce in her sleep, her sweet son, Matt D., compiled an Italian cookbook for a school project when he was in high school. He aptly named it *That's Amore*. We strongly suggested he publish it; alas, he has not yet. This book just may be the impetus he needs.

Matt D.'s Italian heritage is so important to him, especially after he had an epiphany in Italy. It's not a coincidence his children call him "Bobo," which is "Daddy" in Italian. About this sauce, Matt says, "This is a secret recipe, and I actually had trouble putting this in my book. As a gift from me to you, I would like to present you with the passport to my heart: sauce and meatballs. This is no laughing matter. The five Daniels cousins have been known to frequently hide sauce and meatballs, and if you're not in the family, fuhgettaboudit. There's no way you're getting within thirty feet of the pot."

Ingredients
3–4 pounds of pork loin end roast, bone-in; trim fat from pork
1–2 tablespoons of lard
1 clove of garlic
5 12-oz. cans of tomato paste

Directions
- Brown garlic and take it out of the pot.
- Brown pork on all sides.
- Open cans of tomato paste and put in with the meat. Add six 12-oz. cans of water. Mix well.
- Lower heat to medium.
- Add salt to taste.
- If sauce starts to get thick, add more water.
- Cook for 3½ to 4 hours.

Fun footnote: Matt reveals in his book that Kathy's all-time record is frying 321 of Gram's meatballs for a party she was having. Way to go, Kath.

And that, sister-friend, that's amore.

Seventh Stop: Praying
(Friends from Praying)

Prayer helps us anchor our faith in God. It's like setting our spiritual compass so that regardless of the twists and turns during the day, the needle of our focused faith always turns to God.[1]
—Anne Graham Lotz

Sister-friend, this stop contains some serious subject matter (and you'll be thrilled to know the next one does, as well). Not for sissies. Sittin' taller now?

It would greatly behoove us if we donned a pair of hiking boots before getting out of our car. Tall socks first, followed by a quick spritz of bug spray. Not that I'm the great outdoorswoman; we simply must be prepared.

Hiking boots not only protect our feet, they also keep our ankles from twisting. We need all the help we can get, given the mountain we're about to climb. Don't forget we're making the climb *together*, the Lord before us and behind us (Psalm 139:5).

In a spinning/cycling class John and I've taken, the instructor forewarns us, "We're comin' up on a hill." That means the riding will become much more difficult, but once we reach the peak, it's coasting, downhill all the way. This stop will mirror that ride.

Friendly Encounters

You're about to meet some friends who take prayer very seriously. They define prayer warriors. They make praying look like a downhill ride versus an uphill climb.

The Lord introduced me to two wildly important people (WIPs) in a paradise-like location. I ran into both of them in Naples, Florida. Twenty-one years apart.

The first WIP happens to be the devastatingly handsome young man who would become my husband. John and I met on the pier in 1981. We were both students at the University of Kentucky. It just so happened that we both had friends who invited us to go to Naples for spring break. We praise you, Lord.

It's a given that John and I stand on the pier every single time we return to our paradise. Reminiscing never gets old, even three decades later.

Pity our poor children's friends who traveled to Naples with us over the years. We'd drag everyone out onto the pier to show them exactly where our history happened. (Audible groans fell out of our boys' mouths, along with, "Here we go again.")

The second WIP, a lovely woman, just so happened to be

staying next door to our family's condo while we were vacationing at Christmastime one year. She and her husband were also on vacation.

To get to the elevator, they had to walk past our lanai. John and I sip coffee and read on that porch every morning. Our first morning there, the handsome couple smiled and greeted us. The four of us quickly struck up a conversation.

They were from Chicago. We told them we were from Louisville. They told us their names were Dick and Becky, but for some reason, we never got their last name.

Becky said, "You know, I once visited a church in Louisville. It had some directional name, like Northwest."

I asked, "Could it have been Southeast? That's where we attend."

She replied, "Yes, that's it. Might you know the pastor's wife, Judy Russell?"

A bit surprised by her question, I said, "It just so happens she's one of my very dear friends."

Stunned, Becky added, "I haven't talked with Judy in forever. If I write her a note, would you please deliver it to her?"

"Happy to," I said.

We talked some more, and before we knew it, a few days passed, and it was time for Dick and Becky to return to Chicago. John and I had wanted to get to know them better, only barely becoming acquainted.

We were lounging by the pool reading that afternoon when we saw them walk past our porch upstairs.

Becky hollered over the railing, "Hey, I'm leaving this note for Judy on your table. I'm also leaving you some information if you happen to get to Chattanooga next summer, I'm helping with an event there."

And with that, they were gone.

Curiosity overtook me. I bolted up the five flights of stairs to our porch. There was the note for Judy, along with a brochure. Becky turned out to be Rebecca Manley Pippert, the author of the classic, *Out of the Saltshaker and Into the World: Evangelism as a Way of Life.*

Kay Arthur was offering a huge conference in Chattanooga, and Becky was one of the featured speakers. Are you kidding me?

I could hardly wait to get home. That Sunday, thanks to our Great Connector, I ran right into Judy. I could hardly slow down long enough to tell her about meeting Becky, how she never told us who she was, how she'd written a note for her for me to deliver, and how famously the four of us got along, if only for a brief time.

Lean in now, you won't believe this: Judy goes home and reads the note. Becky gave her their phone number. Judy calls her, and they reconnect for over an hour.

Next thing we know, Dick and Becky are coming to Louisville to visit Bob and Judy. One problem: Bob and Judy are tied up for dinner, and Dick and Becky are due to arrive in the afternoon.

Judy asked, "Would you and John entertain them for dinner and then bring them to our house?"

"Oh, yes, ma'am, would we ever," I quickly answered. Something in me told me to "sell them on Kentucky." I have no idea why, but God did.

I whipped up everything Kentucky's known for. We began with warmed melt-in-your-mouth country ham biscuits. Dinner included super Southern-n-creamy cheese grits, complementing beef tenderloin with Henry Baines's sauce (a Louisville specialty, originating at the Pendennis Club). Dessert was the ever reliable and infamous Derby Pie, also originating in Louisville, served à la mode, of course. (You'll find the original recipe for this as well as a gluten-free option on my website.)

We lingered over dinner. Before we knew it, Judy was calling to say she and Bob were home. I guess we chatted a little too long, as Judy had to call us the second time, wondering what was taking us so long to deliver Dick and Becky.

I believe it was the Lord who impressed selling Kentucky upon me because Bob and Judy felt the exact same way. Bob suddenly suggested that Dick and Becky move here and base their ministry out of Louisville. It was as if we were watching dominos, with Dick and Becky perched atop them, tumbling straight for us.

The hurdles they jumped to move to Louisville were equally miraculous. Before we knew it, Dick and Becky, and Becky's son David, along with a very large moving van, arrived in our city. Even better, they now lived a mile up the road from us. Is God unbelievable or what?

During their time in Louisville, in between their ministry trips, Becky, Jane, Doris, and I (you'll get to know them all on this stop) became very close friends. As we watched Dick and Becky's ministry mushroom, someone suggested Becky needed a prayer ministry to cover them wherever they traveled.

The Prayer Warriors were born. Becky's invitation to be prayer warriors for her and her ministry was exciting, yet a first for me. Back then, "bold" would never have been a word to describe my prayer life, thus this was a big uncomfortable yes.

This opportunity made us get serious on the prayer level. That's what prayer warriors do. We dove in, excited, timid, maybe even scared (well, I was), but the operative word was we did this *together*.

Becky reminded us often of Ephesians 6:18–19: "And pray in the Spirit on *all* occasions with *all* kinds of prayers and requests. With this in mind, be alert and always keep on praying for all the Lord's people. Pray also for me, that whenever I speak, words may be given me so that I will fearlessly make known the mystery of the gospel" (emphasis mine). Though Paul wrote these verses, they became our mission to pray for Becky.

The bond the Lord knit between us seared our spirits faster than usual. We gained deep, deep friendships, warrioring together. Those were sacred times. It was as if we prayer warriors had known each other all our lives. "What? You too?" The Lord knew what He was doing. He was about to call Becky to something much bigger.

We learned that ministry, while impactful and uplifting, is not a constant cakewalk. Many of you are nodding. The good news is, we celebrated many beautiful transformations in Becky and Dick's work for the Lord: droves of people were coming to know Him.

Dick and Becky were actively, constantly spreading the gospel via Becky's Bible studies she's written, or sermons she's given, or attendees were being blessed by her prayer ministry after giving a talk. But because their ministry was abroad, numerous challenges began piling up.

Satan was not at all happy with what they were doing. He threw fiery darts from every angle, trying to derail them. These are just a few of those darts: delayed flights, sudden illnesses, lost luggage, even a terrible fall down a dark and dingy basement. Scary.

Time for Becky's prayer warriors to step up the prayers. But while we prayed for Dick and Becky, she would frequently put her needs aside and ask us, "How can I pray for you?" Do you know how silly some of our prayer requests must have sounded? Silly and safe. We had light-years to go to touch Becky's faith, and yet she was and still remains loving, patient, and sincere.

When you think about it, praying is safe. Shauna Niequist says, "Prayer is the safest, most nurturing activity I practice, almost like sitting in the sun, face tilted up, or imagining yourself as a child, crawling up into the lap of a treasured, trusted grandparent."[2] Sometimes when we're together, we do just that, whispering in hushed tones to the God who hears.

In Their Own Words

As you hear from my Prayer Warriors, you'll get to see what it looks like to see Jesus on an airplane; as a friend; in Sunday school; and even in China. You'll be so encouraged.

Encountering the Irresistible Jesus

Let's start with Becky Pippert, my dear friend and faithful prayer warrior. If I could sum up my years of knowing Becky, I'd say she taught me to never give up. Never give up praying, never give up turning over our worries to God, and never stop trusting that the Lord has our best interest at heart, hearing our every request.

She also never, and I do mean *never,* judges anything I report to her. I could've said, "We come from a long line of ax-murderers."

She would not have blinked an eye as she said, "Well, let's get to work, praying how to stop this pattern."

One of Becky's many gifts is making each prayer warrior feel special. She's a relentless listener, wise from years and years of experience, again teaching us more and more about prayer and its power beyond our wildest imaginations. I dare say it's because she's spent so much time sitting at Jesus's feet.

Nothing and no one is too tough or impossible for Becky. Thankfully she passed her fortitude on to our little band of prayer warriors. She always encouraged us to get out of our "holy huddle" and trust in the Lord and His sovereignty so fully that we, too, endeavor to have a smidge of this kind of trust. Watch how Becky handles a total stranger:

> I recently had a lively conversation with a woman sitting next to me on a plane. Our conversation lasted two hours, and we discovered we had much in common: our love of travel, learning about different cultures, reading books, and learning new languages. But our conversation also revealed our very different beliefs: "Listen," she said, "if I want to be a man on Monday and a woman on Wednesday, who cares? At the end of the day, gender identity is simply a matter of personal preference."
>
> She went on to say she believed in the essential goodness of human nature. I asked her how she'd describe the state of the world: "Oh, the world is absolutely falling apart. There's a lot of bad karma floating around out there," she said.

"But how is that possible if the world is filled with good people?" I asked.

She paused and then said, "I believe our problem comes from two sources. Either people have addiction issues and need a recovery program, or they have psychological wounding and need therapy. Don't you agree?" That began a conversation that lasted the entire flight. We talked about culture, and it reminded me of the evangelism I do overseas.

I believe one of the greatest shortcuts to evangelism, apart from establishing genuine friendships with unbelievers, is inviting them to take a fresh look at the Person of Jesus through gospel stories. People who would not darken the door of a church are often curious about who Jesus is, especially if they are approached in the right way.

Why is looking at Jesus through gospel stories so effective? What happened to ordinary people who encountered Jesus in His day? They were amazed by His miracles, astonished by His teaching, shocked by His claims, moved by His tenderness to outsiders and sinners, and stunned by His criticism of religious authorities. This Jesus is so beautiful, so radical, so controversial. He is so much more than words can contain. Jesus always astonished and broke down stereotypes, both then and now.

This is why evangelism, at its core, isn't about techniques or formulas. It's about bringing people into the presence of Jesus. One way to do this is through what we call a Seeker Bible Study: introducing our unbelieving friends to the real Jesus in the gospels, through question-based studies of various passages. The fruit we have seen, both here and around the world, when we teach Christians how to do this (even in a secular place like Europe), has been utterly remarkable.

What Hasn't Changed?

As my new acquaintance on the plane and I grabbed our bags and said goodbye, she suddenly turned around and said, "I'm embarrassed to say this, but I feel very drawn to you, and I so enjoyed our conversation. If I emailed you, would you write me back?"

I assured her I'd be delighted.

To my surprise, she wrote me the very next day.

I wrote her back and said, "I didn't mention this on the plane but I wrote a book called *Hope Has Its Reasons* for people who are seeking God or for something they can't quite name. I am a Christian, so my book comes from that faith perspective. But I want to suggest something else: You told me you'd never read the Bible as an adult. I have written several Bible studies for seekers who want to know more about Jesus. May I send one to you?"

She wrote back immediately and said, "Are you psychic? How did you know I am searching for God? Please send it to me!"

We are now in an email conversation about faith.

Yes, our culture is becoming increasingly secular; the elite voices in our culture are much more hostile and antagonistic to true Christian faith. But secularism doesn't have the power to take away people's longing for meaning, worth, or wholeness.

If anything, it exacerbates their hunger because God has placed in all human beings a longing for meaning and purpose that they can't quite name. But it's there. Yet how will unbelievers know where to look unless Christians live to tell the Best News ever? Finding a way to reach unbelievers and becoming Christians who are outwardly focused and inwardly ablaze with the love of Christ, this is our global challenge! God wants to use us, but will we let Him?

Keep in mind that Becky's been evangelizing for years. She makes it seem simple, and yet isn't it cool how she very gently and matter-of-factly approached the woman on the plane? We don't have to be proficient professors with wisdom pouring out of our mouths. We just need to share the love of Christ—the "global challenge," as Becky says.

Friends with Jesus?

You already met Jane Chilton, the leader of our Abbies, on our third stop. She also happens to be an outstanding prayer warrior. She kept Becky's Louisville Prayer Warriors together, thanks to her fine calendar coordinating and text reminders.

How Jane landed in a Bible study is the essence of her heart for prayer today. Look at what she says about her first Bible study and the many facets of friendship she's gained with the Lord:

I had no idea my life was about to be altered forever in multiple ways. One of the greatest and most unexpected ways my life has changed is by developing a deep, personal friendship with Jesus.

The more I studied the Bible, the better I came to know Jesus for who He really is. The more I came to know the real Jesus, the greater my love for Him became. Really getting to know someone and appreciating who they are and them reciprocating is what true, deep friendship looks like.

My friendship with Jesus now fashions the foundation of my life. This friendship molds my beliefs, opinions, thoughts, and actions. It influences all my other relationships.

Friendship with Jesus gives assurance that you and I will always be loved, all the way through eternity. It also bathes one's life every single second of every single day with grace, mercy, and multiple second chances. Believe me, I constantly need those benefits!

Friendship with Jesus provides a sense of security no human is capable of giving. It provides the experience of total, unconditional love. His friendship provides companionship 24/7.

The great news is I'm not a rare, unique individual who's qualified to experience friendship with Jesus. I'm just a regular woman who said yes to His invitation. Dear friend, He extends the very same invitation to each of us.

From time to time I wonder, "What if I had not said *yes* … to my friend's invitation to come to Bible study … to my Savior's offer of friendship?" Thank God, literally, I said yes!

Jane experienced a big uncomfortable yes, fearing the unknown from joining a new Bible study. You can see the results. The Lord has used her (and is still using her) in multiple and mighty ways, many of us her sheep she faithfully shepherds. Amen.

Sunday School

Our other prayer warrior, while also an Abbie, is Doris Bridgeman. Doris and I go way, way back to when we were both leaders in Bible Study Fellowship (BSF). We attended the very frightening leadership meetings together. Doris impressed me because she was never nervous at those meetings, while the very papers on my lap shook from my knees bouncing up and down.

I placed the meetings in the frightening category because the main teaching leader would randomly choose one of us to lead out the meeting. As a leader, you were to come prepared to lead with a summary sentence or two, ways to introduce the questions, and then lead the group, never knowing if you'd be called on or not. *Not* my cup of tea.

Doris and I reconnected after BSF in a Bible study at Southeast. She, too, had discovered Jane was teaching there. Another, "What? You too?" Later, we both landed on the Women's Council, and because we were both friends with Jane, this led to many lunches out, among other social outings.

I call Doris "Dor" just because. A quiet spirit, Dor is passionate about Bible study. Her entire face lights up when she talks about the Word of God:

> As an adult, I can't imagine not being in Bible study with other ladies to be encouraged and strengthen my faith. But where and when was the root planted that now blooms in me, as I'm still in the study of God's Word today?
>
> My first encounter with learning about God was in Sunday school, a child's version of Bible study. At an early age, God's Word was like a treasure chest, opened

for me. I fondly remember the faithful teachers who helped cultivate and plant seeds in me, showing me how to know Christ and to have a relationship with Him.

Even before I could read, I remember the picture cards with scripture and a story on the back. Proudly I would carry the cards home like they were a prize to show my mom what I'd received, not realizing the true treasure I'd been given. Not only was I introduced to the Word, I was also introduced to the concept of fellowship with my peers as we learned about Jesus while trying to navigate life together. I was given the special gift of kinship with others in the body of Christ, a special sisterhood.

As life has carried me beyond that small church environment, I still carry with me the need and desire to be in community with others as I study God's Word. I must rely on His truths and use them as the path beneath my feet (Psalm 119:105).

The added bonus is that special sisterhood I mentioned. We're blessed through a shared fellowship in Christ, while doing life together.

Every week in Bible study, we Abbies welcome the powerful insights Dor gifts us with. Her dedication is contagious, and it all began with Sunday school.

A Child from China?

Another one of my Abbies caused me to realize that all of them are strong prayer warriors. Reggie Willinger recently opened my eyes from her incredible story you're about to read. (As of this writing, my cell phone is lighting up with prayers about an incoming hurricane that could affect Reggie's son and Olivia's brother. Our prayers fly back and forth, bringing us comfort and urgency to approach our heavenly Father. That's what prayer warriors do.)

Reggie's a dear friend. She also happens to be Gwennie's sister. They beautifully resemble each other and are a hoot to behold.

When Reggie was homeschooling her daughter Cami, she would bring her to Bible study at Jane's. We all hugged her, fighting over who would get to pick her up, always dying to see what precious outfit she'd march in wearing.

Cami brought schoolwork but inevitably wound up in our room. I can't think of a better conversation to eavesdrop into than sentences saturated in scripture, can you?

Enjoy Reggie's amazing story of how God plopped Cami, the cutest little girl from China, in their family's lap. (Don't miss the support of their friends along the way.):

> I've been in Bible study since I was a child. From Sunday school lessons, to church youth group studies and retreats, to large group adult studies and now a small group home study, I have reaped, and continue to reap, the benefits of studying God's Word. It was while I was teaching a children's Sunday school class that God began to open my heart to adoption.
>
> My husband and I already had five children. Andy's company was in the process of being acquired, which meant his future employment was questionable, and we were an older couple, as far as becoming parents was concerned. We had legitimate excuses as to why we should not adopt, but of course, none of them were as powerful as God's reason for why we *should* adopt.
>
> We attended several adoption seminars, but nothing resonated with us. A friend from Bible study said she could see me with a "little China girl" on my hip.

Not long after that insight, God opened doors and placed a weight so heavy on my heart that we were to adopt a little girl from China, I could no longer make excuses.

Andy was a little skeptical at first, but after much prayer, he agreed that if I felt strongly that God was leading us to adopt, he would follow. Throughout this lengthy process, we were blessed to be covered in prayer from our families and the adult and children's Bible study classes we attended.

Several interviews and mountains of paperwork later, we were waiting to receive information on the little girl the Chinese government had chosen for us. Then it was my turn to follow Andy's calling from the Lord. He felt we were meant to change our adoption request form to accept a child with minor special needs.

Originally, we didn't believe we could provide all that a special needs child would require because of our large family. We wanted to be responsible by not taking on more than we could handle. Of course, God had it all handled for us in a better plan. His plan. So I trusted Andy, and we changed the form.

Soon, we received pictures and biographies of special needs children from which we could choose to adopt. While China assigns a child to you if the child is healthy, in the case of special needs children, the Chinese government sends you a group to choose from.

Choosing a child is a grueling decision—one you would anticipate would take a very long time. However, from the minute Andy saw our daughter's picture, he knew she was ours. Our older daughter, who had been praying for a sister for years, left us a note before she went to bed telling us, "Go get her!" We then traveled to China to get Cami, and what a blessing she has been!

Cami has permanent nerve damage in her right arm, but she compensates remarkably well. Most people don't even notice. She's a bright, beautiful fourteen-year-old with a sweet spirit and a huge heart for Jesus.

When she was in kindergarten and first grade, I homeschooled her. Jane graciously opened her home for Cami to study in her spare bedroom while we held Bible study in her living room.

What an amazing group of ladies to support me, but what an even more amazing witness for Cami to see women studying scripture, Bibles in hand. She considers this group of women her friends. When we first started this group, I barely knew any of these women, except for my sister, and now they're some of my dearest friends.

We have celebrated our children's marriages, the births of grandchildren, college and career decisions, as well as changes. We have mourned the loss of parents, spouses, and broken marriages but walked beside each other in those valleys.

Most importantly, we have *prayed* through it all and trusted God's sovereignty. These women are prayer warriors. They are not just my dear friends. They are family. They are my sisters in Christ.

One fun little sidebar to this story is Reggie's daughter, who told Reggie and Andy to "go get" the little girl in China, is named Meggie. She impressed me from the first time I met her. For starters, would you want another sibling thrown into your family just like that? That's a huge deal. Being a content lonely only, I confess I'm not so sure I'd have been so excited. ("Does not share well with others" comes to mind.) Mercy. Forgive me, Lord.

Meggie's excitement was contagious for the whole family, and Cami's arrival into the U.S. of A. was a fever-pitch celebration. All too quickly, Meggie graduated from high school and was bound for the University of Georgia.

The Abbies came up with a stellar idea. We marched out and bought a beautiful, brand-new Bible and had Meggie's name engraved on it. We passed it around our group, writing notes to Meggie where our favorite scriptures are. Then we stuffed it with gift cards to all kinds of fun places Meggie could enjoy once she got to college. She came to one of our Bible studies before she was to take off. We prayed over her, praying she'd meet Christian friends and find a solid church. Then we presented her with her new Bible. This is one of my favorite gift ideas for an incoming freshman.

Inspiration to Go

Start small. When we lived in Lake Forest in Louisville, a new neighbor by the name of Cynthia Kraigthorpe started a prayer group. Funny, this idea had never occurred to me or any of our other neighbors. Sigh.

She began by delivering invitations for us to come for coffee. She also requested we bring our favorite coffee mug. This made for an interesting icebreaker, as one by one, we shared why that particular coffee mug was our favorite.

Cynthia then suggested two excellent ideas:

1. We meet monthly and bring something to donate for a local charity; for example, frozen turkeys in November for Dare to Care.

2. We pray for each other and the rest of our neighbors, helping all of us stay better connected. Cynthia opened our eyes to what's right in front of us, just as Becky was open to her seatmate on the airplane.

Maybe purchase a Bible for a new freshman heading off to college?

Solicit prayers from friends when you're facing a huge decision like Reggie and Andy did.

While we're praying, our next stop will take us one step further into the prayer realm, one where we'll be encouraged to *not* throw in the towel (and I pray, for you, it's a big, bright beach towel for you to sit on. I just can't stay away from the beach too long).

Brace yourself; it's time to gather up some prodigals for our prayer lists.

Crack Up over Pot Roast in a Crock-Pot
(from Mary Lewis)

Mary's a friend who has become family. Her daughter, Diana, and our son, John Jr., are married and recently gifted us with our first grandchild. Claire Elizabeth is the first grandchild on both sides of her family; need I say more?

Mary's not only a great cook; she's hilarious, as you'll see when she tells you why this recipe is called "Cracked Up over Pot Roast in a Crock-Pot." Wait 'til you hear why:

My son-in-law, John Jr., loves my crock-pot roast recipe so much that one day he wanted to give it a try. He said he had a crock-pot. This was prior to him marrying my daughter, so I was not only impressed he wanted to *try* the recipe but that he *owned* a crock-pot. I never thought to ask what size his crock-pot was.

Well, John prepared the roast with all the ingredients one morning, and then off to work he went. He came home from lunch and noticed the juice from the pot roast was all over the counter. He was puzzled because he didn't add any water, like the recipe said. So he didn't think much more about it.

That night, I asked him how the roast turned out, and he said it was good but that the juices kept overflowing. I was puzzled by this. Then I asked him what size his crock-pot was, and he said that it wasn't quite as big as mine. I said that he probably got too big of a roast for his size pot. His key words here were "not quite as big as mine." Remember that.

A while had passed, and the next time I was over at his house, I asked to see his crock-pot. I cracked up laughing! His "not quite as big as mine" crock-pot was actually a mini cheese fondue warmer. The thought of him shoving a two-pound roast into this mini pot brought tears to my eyes. So for Christmas that year, I gave him a full-size crock-pot. I've never seen a young man get so excited over a kitchen appliance.

Ingredients

2- to 3-pound roast (I buy the sirloin tip roast because there's less fat)
1 packet of dry ranch dressing mix
1 packet of dry au jus mix
1 stick of butter
1 jar of whole pepperoncini peppers, drained
1 large onion, thickly sliced (optional)
Carrots and potatoes (optional)

Directions

- Place the roast in a *large* (ha ha) crock-pot.
- Sprinkle the dry ranch and au jus packets over the roast.
- Place the onion slices on the roast and then cover with the peppers (use as many as you like).
- Place the stick of butter on top.
- Cook for 6–8 hours on low.
- I also add carrots and potatoes if you have enough room. Do not add any water.
- It will make plenty of its own juice. Just ask my son-in-law!

Eighth Stop: Persevering (Befriending Prodigals)

The difference between mercy and grace? Mercy gave the prodigal son a second chance. Grace gave him a feast.[1]
—Max Lucado

Let's kick the prayer warrior in us into a higher gear now. We're moving into the challenge of praying for prodigals. Hopefully, you're still sportin' your hiking boots. We've come to the end of the trail, but we're not at the top of the mountain yet. To reach the peak, we must now rock climb. Carefully choosing each step, each rock will hoist us one step closer to the peak.

It's easy to pray for jobs or travel mercies or babies or marriages. But prodigals? They're a whole bucket of worms.

Friendly Encounters

I am blessed to have called the late Kristen Sauder a friend and mentor. Though she was younger than I am, she took me under her praying wing and taught me what persevering prayer looked like. I met her years ago in a Bible study she taught.

I must've been a high-maintenance student, asking enough questions to get Kristen to take me on as a project. No prayer request was too tough for her. She taught me ways to tackle a variety of challenges, and I'm forever grateful.

Praying for prodigals is hands down one of the hardest activities I've been a part of, and one I've often ditched from being flat worn out. Kristen taught me, "Prodigals are simply this: people headed in the wrong direction."[2] She reminds us no one is beyond God's reach.

Those of us who knew Kristen miss her tremendously. She was a wife, a mom, a friend to many, a very patient Bible study teacher, and gifted writer. Her *Further Still Ministries* continues to bless and equip countless people.

It's bittersweet for me to reread Kristen's Bible study she wrote called *Praying for Your Prodigal: A Journey through Luke 15*. One of many encouraging pieces of advice Kristen gives is, "Even if your prodigal remains in the far country, know that God is at work. Don't judge the success of your prayer pilgrimage by the address of your prodigal."[3] Let that soak in for a minute.

In Their Own Words

Kristen taught me so much about praying for prodigals, helping me recognize that "What? You too?" look many of my friends have had over the years. You know, the look a friend gives when they can't hide their pain. The tears in their eyes, the head-shake of disbelief. The discouragement in their tone.

I've met several people praying for prodigals over the years. We're about to be blessed from testimonies from experts. I don't consider myself an expert, although I'll be sharing an only-God-could-pull-this-off kind of story, plus there's a friend who persevered for her wayward husband, and one who learned from putting pen to paper, all the while praying nonstop.

When God Reaches Down

I was a casebook text of a prodigal. Reminders of those prodigal years resurfaced a few years ago. Because right about the time you think the Lord's not paying attention, He proves otherwise.

John and I were in a season where we were buried by our calendars. The weekly challenge became "How can we get our three boys to their sporting events at different times, in different locations, and in different cities?" We were like soulless, helpless robots. Look what the Lord did to wake me up:

Being a consummate planner, last-minute invites generally don't fly with me. However, a few years ago, a long lunch with a mentor of mine birthed a last-minute invite to go to Nashville for the weekend.

This invitation resulted in an uncomfortable yes because I figured there'd be no way I could squeeze in an escape. Remember our family's perpetually swamped season. Clearly, God opened up a window for me to temporarily fly the coop.

I joined seven other gals, most of whom were on staff at Southeast Christian Church (SEC). We were off and running to attend a women's ministry conference at the Opryland Hotel in Nashville. Yes! Another road trip.

We met at Starbucks at eight o'clock sharp. Early morning drives demand large quantities of caffeine. Our leader, Lynn Reece, had quite the agenda in mind, with numerous stops. You'll be stunned to hear shopping bags began to accumulate in the back of our cars.

Round about five o'clock in the evening, our caravan finally hit the Briley Parkway. John called to check on us. He was aghast to discover what normally would've been a three-hour drive took us nine hours. Hey, a girl's gotta do what a girl's gotta do.

The Opryland Hotel was bustling with people. Our conference alone had about two thousand women in attendance. There were a couple other similar-sized conferences going on simultaneously. Thus the "human terrarium," as Eric Metaxas dubs the hotel, was bursting at the seams.

All eight of us were thrilled to have the opportunity to hear from several excellent speakers. The next morning before the program, the beautiful emcee headed straight for me.

She said, "Don't I know you from somewhere?"

I looked to my left and right, certain she couldn't possibly be speaking to me.

"Don't I know you from somewhere?" she repeated.

Finally, I said, "Are you talking to me?"

"Yes," she replied. "I just know I know you from somewhere."

We began working backward. She lives in Bowling Green. I live in Louisville. College? Now we were getting somewhere: We both attended the University of Kentucky. Sorority? We were both members of Kappa Alpha Theta. At about the same time.

Then, as if time stood still, God removed the scales from my eyes, ears, and heart. He showed us we were at the University of Kentucky, at the same time, in the same sorority. Indeed, I did remember her. She was Pam Waldrop, one of the UK cheerleaders.

Where we differed, I'm sad to report, was in our faith. Pam was part of what we then called the God Squad. You probably remember I was not.

But God—oh, you knew that was coming—God stopped me in my tracks, right there in the middle of the conference. Exhibiting grace, Pam didn't bring up those bad memories. Instead, as if God Himself spoke these words, Pam poured out pure grace.

"Elizabeth! Don't you see?" she said. "We're not only sorority sisters; now we're spiritual sisters, daughters of the King."

Endless tears began to flow. God rescued and redeemed me, in a sea of thousands of women and other conference attendees, right smack dab in the middle of the Opryland Hotel.

Keep your eyes open; you never know where He'll rescue you. He delights in second chances. All praise and glory goes straight to you, Lord. Amen.

Isaiah 46:4 depicts my only-God-could-pull-this-off experience at the gigantic, full-of-people, Opryland Hotel: "Even to your old age and gray hairs I am He, I am He who will sustain you. I have made you and I will carry you; I will sustain you and *I will rescue you*" (emphasis mine).

The Lord guided Pam to show me He knew all along the path I would take. He opened my eyes to see the past is, well, passed. Sheer grace and forgiveness cover us both. Not judgment. Hallelujah.

Footnote: One crucial detail you must know is my friend Jane was also supposed to go on this trip. Something prevented her from going at the last minute, which nearly made me bail. (Yet another piece to my uncomfortable yes.) She assured me I could be a big girl and go. I phoned her after my reunion and conversation with Pam, saying, "Now I know why I was supposed to be here. You're never going to believe this …"

God is good. All the time.

My experience at Opryland became a huge spiritual marker in my life. I wrote it down quickly in my Bible. Spiritual markers are the gargantuan boosts we all need to persist in praying for prodigals.

Mary Neal, in her book *7 Lessons from Heaven*, calls her spiritual markers "Ebenezers." She shows us readers 1 Samuel 7:12 where Samuel names his stone Ebenezer (meaning "stone of help"). This enabled him to remember when the Lord helped him and the Israelites have victory over the Philistines. The stone was a tangible reminder.

When Your Husband Is a Prodigal

This next story could also be called an Ebenezer. I want to tell you about my friend who has an astonishing testimony. Her name is

Cassie Soete. The first time I heard her story, I immediately blurted out while shaking my head, "There is no way I'd have hung in there."

Cassie and I met through Bible studies and the book club. When I tell you Cassie and her husband, George, blew up the Marriage Mentoring Ministry at Southeast, I mean that in a good way. There was rarely any marriage they couldn't help repair (with the Lord's hand and a truckload of prayer, of course).

Cassie claims she's much older than I am, but the evidence simply isn't there. She's way cool, always looks like a million bucks, juggles a boatload of adorable grandchildren, while blessing anyone in her path.

Cassie's journey has been mostly wonderful, but her detour from a straight and smooth road involved her husband...

On our twentieth anniversary, George informed me he was leaving me to marry someone else, who happened to be a close friend. That was the first shocker, coupled with the fact our six children ranged in age from two to nineteen.

Somehow I prayed nonstop for George. For four and a half years, he came in and out of our lives eight times, each time saying he was home for good.

I hit the wall after the four-year mark. Anger took over, and I had a little chat with God. I told Him He would have to be the one to fix our marriage, that I was done trying.

That was the beginning of the total strength I found in my awesome God. My faith became immovable with every step I took, with every breath I breathed. Philippians 4:13, "For I can do everything through Christ, who gives me strength" (NLT) became a promise I still rely on every day of my life.

I told George he'd have to earn his divorce every step of the way because my "until death do us part" vow would not be broken on my account. This made him accountable for the first time in his life.

George began to see the changes in me and how my faith was an integral part of my life. One day, he heard something I was saying about Jesus, and he said, "I want what you have," meaning my faith.

One night, while George was unable to sleep in his apartment, he reached for the Bible the children and I had given him for Christmas. He was so convicted, he asked the Lord to come into his life. He never once looked back.

Our faithful, awesome God restored our broken marriage to the fullest. Our loving, giving God became the center of our marriage, such an amazing fifty-plus years to spend with the love of my life. God showed His power by reuniting two broken souls to help others heal their marriages.

My life has changed again: My precious George went to be with the Lord on April 7, 2015. I am blessed to have shared eighteen thousand four hundred and sixty-two days with my sweet husband. I see after one year of being alone that God continues to be my awesome God. He lifts me up even now as I write these very difficult words. He has never left my side. He's the hope I cling to as the children and I grieve the loss of such a godly man.

Cassie's husband, George, is a huge spiritual marker/Ebenezer for so many. Cassie and George's son, Jeff, is actually mentoring our son, John Jr., and several other young men in the Man Challenge

Bible Study at Southeast. George's legacy lives on. We praise you, Lord.

When Cassie and George celebrated their fiftieth anniversary, they were a living example of Psalm 85:10: "Lovingkindness and truth meet together; Righteousness and peace kiss each other. Truth springs forth from the earth, and righteousness looks down from heaven."[4] Their celebration is a tender memory.

Pray as Often as You Breathe

In addition to praying for prodigals, another tool is necessary; it's a word I hesitate to throw out because there are those in this camp and then there are others who shut down at the mere mention of it. I'm about to introduce you to someone who is more than an authority on the subject, thanks to her mother, and that's Olivia Sauder Mitchell. (Yes, she's one of Kristen's children.) The word? Journaling.

My guess is you'll be swayed to try journaling, if you're not already a journaler. Olivia is a precious newlywed, seminary student, and prayer warrior:

> Growing up, we prayed all the time. Before school, my entire family would get on our knees around the coffee table and pray for certain things, depending on the day of the week. We prayed in the car before work, church, school, or any event. If someone was having a hard day, or when something super exciting happened, we prayed to either ask for help or praise God for answered prayer.
>
> It was not uncommon at all to just pause to pray at any time during the day. I cannot remember one time while I was away at college that I spoke with either of my parents on the phone, that they didn't pray for me at the end of the conversation.

New carpool kids from the neighborhood learned quickly that no matter how sleepy we were, on the way to school, we prayed. I love that I grew up in a home where prayer was so common and so natural. Now that I'm married and beginning a family, I am so grateful that this spirit of continued prayer has carried throughout my life.

One of the hardest areas people typically find to be consistent in prayer is when praying for something or someone who doesn't seem to change. Praying for a prodigal is the best example I can think of that's often so difficult to remain faithful.

My mom was one of the best and most consistent prayer warriors I knew. She never gave up; she kept pleading with the Father to draw lost ones back to Him. One way she guarded against losing hope was through journaling. Any time she saw fruit, no matter how small, she would record it in her journal.

Often when praying for prodigals, you get to move one step forward, but then fall two steps back. Those recorded answers to prayer help you remember that God is bigger than your fears, and they will help you not give up in your prayers. Galatians 6:9 has been so helpful for me on this point: "Let us not become weary in doing good, for at the proper time we will reap a harvest if we do not give up."

My mom is in heaven, but I believe the prayers she prayed on earth for her family and other prodigals continue. She never gave up, even when conflicts arose and progress seemed nonexistent. Although she did not get to see the final fruit from her labor of prayer, I believe she will one day.

> You never know how your prayers today will be answered tomorrow. Don't give up, for one day we will reap a harvest.

Sister-friend, I dare you to try arguing with Olivia. Remember the "stone of help" from 1 Samuel 12? Mary Neal calls her journal her "memory book." Assuming we now have our journals, they can be our very own "personal collection of Ebenezer stones."[5]

On a shallow note, next time you're shopping, check out the each-one-is-so-pretty-how-can-one-decide variety of journals available. They're so appealing, they'll win your affection and, I pray, your own words. Ready?

Inspiration to Go

Let's rewind the benefits from persevering in prayer:

We experience many facets of friendship, receive encouragement, and log proof into our journals. Answered prayers keep us refueled to continue praying, growing our faith, bringing us that much closer to the Lord Jesus. He told His disciples "it was necessary for them to pray consistently and never quit" (Luke 18:1 MSG).

The greatest blessing comes if the prodigal for whom you've been praying lives in your city. When they return to the Lord and you get to see them many times afterwards, it's a visual answer to prayer and precisely what we need to persevere.

Case in point: I have a young prodigal whom I prayed for, for years. She surprised all of us when she called her family to bring her home. Why should we be surprised when that was precisely what we'd been praying for all along? She has no idea how encouraged I am each and every time I'm with her. We praise you, Lord.

Two of our very dear, longtime friends are Mark and Michelle Wheeler. Mark and I worked together at Citizens Fidelity Bank (now PNC) many moons ago. He and Michelle came to our wedding in

1984, toting their four-week-old daughter, Erin. I still call her "Miss Erin." Erin's another visual answer to prayer, having gone through some very difficult prodigal years.

She and her husband and her parents credit the Healing Place here in Louisville with her homecoming. What a saving grace, quite literally, and how very thankful we are for miracles. We praise you, Lord.

Our sense of community becomes stronger when praying for prodigals.

We remind each other to pray and keep praying.

My favorite reminder is straight out of scripture: The Holy Spirit will intercede for you when you're too tired so you can pick up where you left off later. As we read in Romans 8:26, "In the same way, the spirit helps us in our weakness. We do not know what we ought to pray for, but the Spirit himself intercedes for us through wordless groans."

Lucky you, our last two stops plunge us into our own kin and into those who are practically kin. Some of you groan when you hear the word "family," while others relish spending time with their relatives. Regardless, I promise we'll have some fun.

Join me as we perch on our family tree.

Two Equally Tasty Variations on Grilled Salmon

This first recipe is from our neat-n-fun neighbors in Naples, Florida. They hail from Chicago but wisely winter in Naples. When we visit, we have nearly daily morning coffee sessions and solve many of everyone's woes. Their names are Shelley and Ron Holt. Ron is the quintessential griller.

The first time he served this salmon, we begged mercilessly for the recipe. Everyone we've made this for, including six for six of our kids, adore this dish, and then they begged for the recipe.

This one is a marinade, while the second recipe's variation is a dry rub. Again, if John and I can make this work, you can too. Done deal.

Foolproof Marinade
Marinade
⅔ cup maple syrup
2 tablespoons fresh lime juice
2 tablespoons salad oil
2 tablespoons soy sauce
1 tablespoon Dijon mustard
Garlic to taste
2 pounds of salmon will give you 4 ample servings

Directions
- Mix up the marinade in a bowl. Slice the two pounds of salmon, keeping the skin on, into 4 or more servings. Using a large baggie, place the salmon in, skin side down. Pour marinade over the salmon, and marinate about an hour.
- Fire up the grill, getting it to be on high heat, 500 or more degrees. Cover a grilling dish with aluminum foil. Place salmon on it, skin side down. Grill for 14 minutes. No more. No less. Enjoy.

Delectable Dry Rub

Ya-Ya Denise served the Yas-n-Yos this salmon dish one night. We loved it so much, we all marched out the next day and purchased the ingredients for the rub, plus enough cedar planks to build a tree house.

Denise also taught us that while the recipe for the rub is only enough for four servings, if you keep doubling it up to make a bunch, it keeps well in a plastic container. Then when you're ready to grill again, just pull out that container of the rub, and you're ready to go.

Ingredients
Dry Rub
- 1 tablespoon brown sugar
- 1 tablespoon coarse salt
- 2 teaspoons ancho chili powder
- 1 teaspoon ground cumin (Denise uses half this amount because her hub's not too wild about cumin; personal preference.)
- ½ teaspoon black pepper (Here in Kentucky, bourbon-smoked salt, pepper, cayenne, and then some, are hot commodities. They are all wonderful. I use them on just about everything, just FYI.)

Salmon
- 4 6-oz. salmon filets
- 1 cedar grilling plank
- Honey for drizzling

Directions
- Presoak a cedar plank at least one hour or more prior to grilling.
- Preheat grill to medium-low heat, about 350 degrees.
- In a small mixing bowl, pour in all of the rub ingredients.
- Rinse salmon off, and pat dry.

- Generously sprinkle rub ingredients all over the salmon and set aside.
- Place the presoaked cedar plank on the grill, close the lid, and heat for 3 minutes. (Be sure to keep an eye on the plank, as we've all torched a few.)
- Using tongs, turn the plank over and place the salmon on the heated side of the plank. Close the grill lid and grill for 12–15 minutes or until desired doneness.
- Remove the planked salmon and drizzle with desired amount of honey. (Don't forget the honey. I did one time, and it just wasn't the same. By the time I realized it, it was too late.)
- Serve immediately.

Footnote: The combo of the spices and the honey is what sets this recipe apart. People go bonkers. Just try it.

Ninth Stop: Shopping and Cheering (Friends with Kin)

I'm a shopaholic on the road to recovery. Just kidding. I'm actually on the road to the mall.[1]

Never in my wildest dreams did I imagine John and I would one day be blessed with three daughters-in-love. Submerged in my perpetually all-male world of one adventurous husband plus three sons, escape seemed improbable. Mere survival was a major accomplishment.

Once our three boys were old enough to go to dances in high school, our shopping outings wrapped up in five minutes flat: one new tie or a pair of khakis. Finito.

The boys passed down navy blazers, which made splurging for another a rarity. Wildly exciting.

Friendly Encounters

Enter girlfriends, followed by fiancées, blossoming into brides-to-be. Our daughters-in-love were most gracious and invited me to shop for wedding dresses (heavenly), go on birthday shopping trips (a newfound exercise inspired by my brilliant cousin), get mani-pedis together, and learn how to apply cosmetic masks during family vacation (while frightening our husbands). These darling girls, Diana, Lauren, and LT (short for Lindsey-Taylor), take shopping to a whole new level. I realize I've been in the dark for thirty plus years.

Our girls have helped me more than once when I wallow in the I-don't-have-anything-to-wear woes. They can talk the night away, while shopping the day away. They sniff out bargains like our 2,000 percent terrier, Gracie, sniffs out bacon.

Charles Lamb nailed our chatter when he said, "Tis the privilege to talk nonsense, and to have her nonsense respected." Yes.

One bit of nonsense blessed me not too long ago. I've since shared it with my girls. Priscilla Shirer admitted she has a bizarre attachment to belts. She hauled the biggest bunch of belts up on stage at a conference once, claiming she has a "shopping anointing." I'm afraid my husband would place me in that category as well, now knowing we girls can save our husbands so much money. I digress.

Each of our daughters-in-love holds a special place in my heart. To experience their thoughtfulness and see their love and affection for our sons is over-the-top wonderful. For me to gain daughters, who I also consider sweet sister-friends, I can't think of anything more cherishable. Another gift from God.

I recently learned about a concept I'd like to share with you. It's about each of us becoming a balcony person. Since our shared pursuit at this stop is shopping and cheering, you and I will cheer on friends and family sans cheerleading uniforms. Whew.

The petite-yet-powerful book that taught me about this concept is entitled *Balcony People by* Joyce Landorf Heatherley. Joyce teaches us balcony people have the gift of affirmation, cheering others on.

Joyce asks, "Who is the special affirmer who catches quick glimpses of the flames from the fires of your potential and *tells* you so? Who, by his or her words, helps you to respect and believe in your own value as a person?"[2]

She reminds us how crucial it is for us to cheer each other on. After all, we witness cheering throughout the Bible. We're commanded to and called to love one another (John 13:34–35).

As you meet some of my family who are also friends in this chapter, keep your friends in mind too, thinking of how you can cheer them on. These family members are gifted balcony people.

They share the three traits of a balcony person, according to Joyce: "They love, listen, and care from the heart."[3]

Let's take a peek now into those who I try to cheer on and who, in turn, most definitely cheer me on. Let's return to our little family.

The summer before our granddaughter, Claire Elizabeth, was born, we coordinated all eight of our calendars to go on a family vacation to Gulf Shores, Alabama (miracles can still happen).

As we discussed the importance of the table thanks to Judy's input on our fourth stop, the table played a large role in our family vacation, as well. The condo where we stayed had my favorite kind of table: a round one, for eight. The huge brandy snifter filled with sand, shells, and starfish made for a beautiful centerpiece. Yes, we were blissfully and frequently found gathered around that table.

Each couple took a night to cook. Our family room, kitchen,

and dining area were all one, so we could watch our chefs at work. Thankfully, each couple offered appetizers, because the aromas coming from the kitchen caused us all to want to grab a sample before the dinner bell rang. (I'm guessing spatulas would've warmed our knuckles had we tried to snatch anything too early.)

Our grill got a workout too. We savored fish tacos, chicken with avocado and tomato, and sumptuous, thick-n-juicy steaks. All the girls are creative in the culinary department, while our boys are great grillers. John and I just stood by and surveyed these babies, now men, now husbands with wives. Someone, please tell me where the time goes.

Each morning on our balcony, various children would surface, with a cup of hot coffee in hand. We soaked in the warm air, watching the waves break on the beach. Eight for eight of us breathed in the salt air. You could see a spirit of relief and peace wash over our faces, brief respites from the wild world from which we'd just escaped.

Our seven days slipped by before we knew it. Summer of 2017 took us to South Carolina, this time toting a new, pink granddarlin' with us to Wild Dunes, which lived up to its name. Charleston and the Isle of Palms delighted us with shrimp and grits, fun shopping (oh, yes), and hot temps on the beach. Memories and nine for nine of us remain perched in each other's balconies.

This wasn't always so. Growing up without siblings, I always got along swimmingly by myself (there's something to brag about). After I became a mom, our three boys began saying ridiculous things to each other such as, "He's looking at me," with frightening frowns plastering their faces. This frustrated me immensely.

None of their ridiculing bothered John. He's the baby of four, and such nonsense was just that, nonsense. I simply wanted everyone to keep the peace. A thousand and one times, John's response would be, "Just let it go." Hmph.

Now that our boys are grown and married, they're all really good friends. We praise you, Lord. All three couples traveled together to

New York City for a fun pre-Christmas weekend before Claire was born. This thrilled us.

For the first time in three years of LT and Lauren teaching in two different cities, they had the same spring break. This time, the girls and their hubbies took off for California. John and I got to live vicariously through their stops in Los Angeles, Laguna, and San Diego. (Had Diana not been eight months' pregnant, I'm fairly sure she and John Jr. would've joined them.) Triple joy. Balcony people.

In Their Own Words

As you meet some of my family members, watch for their words of wisdom on prayers from the cradle; the value of experiences over things; family from church; and patient endurance. You'll see why they're so special.

Prayers from the Cradle and Onward

Long before any of our kids were of marrying age, I learned the hard way that offering the slightest hint of approval when your child is dating someone is the kiss of death. This happened to my friend's daughter and our oldest son when they were in middle school. Granted, they were too young anyway, but she and I were thrilled our kids were interested in one another. We made the grave error of letting them know how happy we were about that. Next thing we knew, it was over.

The very same thing began stirring with the daughter of another friend of mine and our youngest son, Woody. This young woman, LT, and Woody began "talking." Christmas came and went, and their high school winter ball was upon us. Woody invited LT to be his date. Her mother, Aletia, and I didn't say a word.

Prior to the winter ball, our home, which had a long staircase with a vaulted ceiling, was the place of choice for taking pictures. Loads of parents and kids began arriving. How we squeezed so many families in one place while taking pictures was baffling. Somehow, it worked.

As if orchestrated, couples filed from the living room to the family room to the stairs, and within minutes, photos were snapped, and poof! They were all gone. Our neighbors must've thought we'd hosted the shortest party in history.

My favorite thing was seeing the girls' dresses, updos, flowers, and impossible-to-walk-in-but-oh-so-chic high heels. The boys' suits were, well, suits.

One super sneaky rendezvous occurred while pictures were still being taken. Unable to discuss Woody's new "date" until now, Aletia and I spotted each other and dashed around the corner to talk. We both did the happy dance. Had our children witnessed this, they would've been horrified, plus we'd have been totally busted by our approval. All we concluded was, "Let's pray." Praise the Lord, in, the summer of 2014, LT and Woody married on the heels of their college graduation.

Aletia and I call each other "SFAM" (Sister from Another Mother). She and I attend Bible study together. She's also an uber faithful prayer warrior, but I thought she should go in this chapter since we're really related now.

At LT's bridal shower, we went around the room and each guest offered a fun story about LT to help us know her better. Audrey told of a time when LT was at their home, spending the night with her daughter, Michelle.

Her son Matt, who's normally pretty quiet, chimed in as someone had said something not-so-nice about LT that day. He said, "No, no, no. LT is an angel. And her mom? She's a really, really big angel." Matt was cheering Aletia on without realizing it.

How true. Those of you who know Aletia are nodding. I often say, "Nobody's *that* nice. But she really is."

Mary says you can see the Holy Spirit in Aletia. I love that. We all need friends like her. Her own words will explain:

Elizabeth and I share our passion and love for our Lord and Savior Jesus Christ. We believe God's Word is our truth serum that rewallpapers our minds and transforms our hearts into who we are in Christ.

Corrie Ten Boom wrote, "What wings are to a bird and sails are to a ship, so is prayer to the soul."[4] Prayer is our direct connection to our loving God. Through studying His Word and being led by the Holy Spirit, we can walk freely into His presence, laying and leaving our prayers and petitions at the foot of the cross.

When my daughters, Chelsea and LT, were young, God placed an idea on my heart to start praying for their future husbands and their families. Philippians 4:6 was our guide: "Do not be anxious about anything, but in every situation, by prayer and petition, with thanksgiving, present your requests to God."

My husband and I are so blessed by our sons-in-love, Woody and Jonathan. We attribute these marriages as answers to prayer, proving there's power in prayer. [4]

The Thompson family is tight-knit. Prayer, plus the fact they're all in each other's balconies, is their common thread. I am so thankful to not only be related to this family, but to call them friends.

Experiences over Things

It just so happens the mother of another one of our daughters-in-love has become a close friend. Her name is Pam Stein Van Arsdall. Her precious daughter, Lauren, is married to our middle son, Gordy.

Pam and her husband, Alan, live in Nicholasville. It's been our joy over the years getting to know them and their extended family.

Recently retired from dentistry, both practicing and teaching at UK's Dental School, Pam enjoys gardening and has started a fascinating website: www.amilliongodstories.com, pointing readers to beautiful testimonies about God, further spreading His daily work in the lives of others.

Early into her parenting, Pam had a huge aha moment. You'll see it's a wonderful idea for all of us, regardless of the ages of our children:

> In 1999, when my daughter, Lauren, was about to turn seven years old, I stood in the middle of our spare bedroom. It had been overtaken by the kids' toys. Completely surrounded by a sea of Lincoln logs, Barbies, a pirate ship, a play kitchen, board games, puzzles, and more, the thought of coming up with a birthday present for my daughter, the thought of buying one more thing made me sick.
>
> That's when I decided to start a new tradition for birthdays: We would *do* something, not *buy* something. Surprisingly, Lauren was on board with this idea.
>
> Each year, we had so much fun researching places we'd like to visit. Together, we'd look for places to stay, sites to see, and restaurants to eat. Sometimes these places were near our home, and we could do a day trip. Other times, the trips were across the country, and we stayed one to two nights.
>
> These were the must-haves of each trip:
> 1. Something educational; we've visited botanical gardens, museums, historical sites, and national parks.
> 2. Read the city map (remember paper maps?) and take public transportation: city bus, the subway, a river boat, a taxi, or a train (this proved to be somewhat adventurous and one time downright dangerous).

3. Eat at one really nice restaurant so that Lauren could learn to appreciate fine food (I surely wasn't cooking like that) and learn proper manners: which fork to use and other confusing niceties.
4. Spend uninterrupted time together, just the two of us.

There wasn't much time in our day-to-day life for me to really get to know her, to really listen to her and learn about her fears, what made her laugh, and her favorite music. Each trip brought new insights for me. Each trip, our mother-daughter relationship transformed a bit more into a deep friendship.

In 2016, my daughter turned twenty-four, and we took a road trip to Austin, Texas, with a pit stop in Waco to see Chip and Joanna Gaines's Silo at Magnolia. It was one of our favorite adventures. Alas, I no longer enforce the paper map requirement for our trips. Instead, we use the iPhone app for directions (which, by the way, got us lost).

I am so thankful for that tiny crowded starter home nearly twenty years ago that forced me to think outside of the box and do something different—something that has become such a sweet, fun tradition.

PS. In case you're wondering, I also took my son John on birthday trips too. We've been to nearly every Major League Baseball field in America.

Pam, Lauren, John, and Alan all cheer for each other. They're clearly in each other's balconies. The Lord answered long-ago prayers to bring Lauren and her family into ours.

New Family from Church

While we're still on this family thread, I discovered that marrying into the Hoagland family came with many benefits. I'd always wanted an older brother. Voilà! There was Billy. Plus, I got not one but two older sisters. They were married, so two more older brother-in-loves, plus Billy's wife, Marte, also became my sister-in-love.

Marte hails from a small town very close to Lexington, where I grew up. (Woodford County touches Fayette County. Woodford County is also home to the city of Versailles, the very same one where the castle is that the Butter Babes visited. Yes indeedy, they say, "Vur-sayelles" too.)

Billy and Marte's kids are stairsteps to ours, which makes the whole cousin thing a sight to behold. Now our babies are having babies, and the Hoagland family is exploding, which is about the most fun thing ever to experience.

I jokingly say Billy rues the day they moved back to Louisville from Indy, where he did his residency. Those were the days when our boys fell out of trees and broke their arms or needed stitches or some wild kind of medical attention (e.g., who falls down steps and bites all the way through their tongue? That would be Woody.).

We called Billy on a weekly basis for years. This was before the days of caller ID, or he may have not answered. Thankfully, he stayed in the medical field, even though we nearly wore him out.

Marte was one of the four friends to invite me to the Bible study I talked about on our third stop. You may recall I turned her down. (Sorta symbolic of our faith walks, as she's always been light-years ahead of me.) I remember calling Marte from a Kroger parking lot one time when I had no idea how to handle a situation; she answered me with lightning speed and Bible verses to back up her answer.

She and Billy recently helped start a church. They've jumped in feet first, serving in every capacity you could think of. Throne of Grace Community Church is something you don't want to miss, if you live in or are close to Louisville. Pop in and tell Pastor Jay Roy a Butter Babe sent you.

Marte's going to explain how their church has become family to them. This is a sweet transformation, where you may see yourself if you've ever helped start a church or joined a new church, most definitely cheering each other on. This is a huge uncomfortable yes Marte and Billy underwent:

A funny thing happened on the way to church one summer night: I realized I was actually excited about going. For weeks that summer, Billy and I would drive out of our neighborhood, jealously waving to friends who were walking their dogs and gathering to have a little hang time with their neighbors before firin' up the grill.

My imagination flew into overdrive. I pictured them shaking their heads and wondering why we felt the need to go back to church to be with all the people we had just spent the morning with. I'd been wondering the same thing until that particular night, when the former "duty" of attending our Sunday night gathering turned into a "desire" to spend time with our church family.

Our pastor promised this would happen. We were part of a handful of people God had given the same vision and desire to take part in a church plant, but we were little more than acquaintances.

Faithfully teaching that first year of what the early church of Acts was like, our pastor helped us reconsider our preconceived ideas of what being part of the church really meant. Truth be told, we all had different ideas, wants, and stubborn sticking points. We were sure of one thing only: that God had drawn us to be on this faith journey together, and we were in it for the duration.

So we examined the scriptures together, sat under our pastor's Christ-exalting teaching, and committed to meet regularly outside of Sunday morning worship to discuss the sermon, pray, disciple each other, and even play.

We met on Sunday nights, Wednesday nights, one-on-one for coffee, and planning meetings on Saturdays. Whew! As we grew closer, we began to share our true feelings about gathering so often.

We grumbled, teased each other about grumbling, laughed at our common reasons for grumbling, and then prayed for each other's lack of gratitude for this blessing. It was akin to a boot camp for spoiled Christians. We all know what happens at a successful boot camp: uniting around a common goal, we became family.

A funny thing happened to our young church as it has grown over the last few years: we see new members begin to struggle with discarding their old ideas about how much is enough church, and we smile, go alongside them, and promise them that they too will soon feel like family.

Billy and Marte's new church has not always experienced smooth sailing. While they've held it together, they've encountered growing pains, no thanks to Satan's disappointment in another church popping up. I am thrilled to report Throne of Grace Community Church just celebrated its fifth anniversary. We praise you, Lord.

Because Throne of Grace's members didn't throw in the towel, persevering as one family, the only thing missing is an actual balcony in their little church. It's there spiritually, though; no worries.

Patient Endurers

One more family member I can't leave out is our brother-in-love, John Rulketter (J.R.), God rest his soul. He was the best kind of friend to my John, which touched me deeply. He was the Steady Eddie in the office where they worked together, many times being a peacemaker as an added bonus (translates into a cheerleader for certain).

After an eight-and-a-half-year battle with melanoma, J.R., as we all called him, went to be with the Lord. His wife, Margee, my John's sister, keeps his legacy alive, as do his children. He's one we all quote often. J.R.-isms are the best (e.g., "It is what it is."), plus we excitedly look forward to reuniting with him in heaven. (I suppose you can be in one's balcony even when they get to heaven first.)

One petite uncomfortable yes occurred the morning after J.R. died. My cell phone lit up with a text just before six o'clock in the morning. Margee asked if I'd help her write J.R.'s obituary. Gulp.

I was already up and big-time prayed for help while dashing down the stairs. Somehow, we completed the obituary, honoring J.R. in a beautiful way.

My favorite phrase Margee suggested was, "John patiently endured the cancer before being ushered into heaven." This was inspired by James 1:12 in the NLT, which says, "God blesses those who patiently endure testing and temptation. Afterward they will receive the crown of life that God has promised to those who love him."

While J.R.'s cancer was a big detour for our family, Margee has encountered another one. She's dealing with Parkinson's. She's patiently enduring the disease and doing so with amazing grace and a rock-solid faith. She lives life to the full with her children and grandchildren. Look out if you get her toes a-tappin'. She is one dancing machine. We praise you, Lord.

To the Rescue

John's oldest sister, Van, is the granola bar of the family (I say this with love and jest). I call her "Vannie." God bless Vannie, she came over before one of our boys' weddings because I was having a hair emergency, of all things. Toting products I didn't know existed, she came to the rescue, swiftly swooping up my mousy hair. She does those kinds of things for friends and family.

Besides being a retired schoolteacher, Vannie's also the quintessential storyteller. When our boys were little and Vannie was over for dinner, she'd instruct them to turn the lights out.

She'd declare, "I've got a new ghost story."

Our boys clung to every word she uttered. Many of those nights, they wound up sleeping on the floor in our room.

Also a mom of boys, Vannie and I have traded a few male tales. We are definitely in each other's balconies.

The Resurrection of Adeline

All four Hoagland children (my John and his three sibs) inherited the artistic gene from their mother, Adeline. Addie is an artiste extraordinaire. Her beautiful oil paintings adorn all of our homes. I love it when people ask me where these paintings came from, and I can answer, "My mother-in-love painted them." What a bonus, right?

Addie's the matriarch of our family. She keeps us gathering for meals, remembers countless birthdays (now having grandchildren and greatgrandchildren), and cheers for all of us while maintaining a social life none of us can touch.

One Saturday morning, much to our dismay, Addie woke up and had trouble speaking. John and I dashed over to their house, meeting the ambulance. A quick assessment confirmed our fears. Addie had had a stroke, and it was a big one. She couldn't talk and couldn't move any portion of the right side of her body.

Oh, but the Lord showed up. Billy is rarely at the hospital on Saturdays, but that day, he was there doing a couple of cases. He met the ambulance and expedited his mother into the emergency room. There also just happened to be a stroke neurologist on call and he was there in five minutes

A quick CT scan showed multiple clots. The doctor said, "If she doesn't have surgery, she'll die. But if she does have surgery, she also may die."

Within minutes, we were told to say our goodbyes. Seeing John's dad tell his beloved wife of nearly seven decades goodbye tore us all up, nurses included.

A few very long hours later, the doctor came out smiling. He had pictures of three clots he'd retrieved. He informed us any one of those could've killed her. We went back into the recovery area and found Addie with a big smile on her face.

She waved to us with the hand and arm that couldn't move hours before, and she spoke to each of us, calling us by name. She is a miracle, for which we are so grateful to the Lord. We've since dubbed this frightening experience "the Resurrection of Adeline." We praise you, Lord.

When John and I look back upon those years of moving my parents multiple times in Lexington and then finally over here to a nursing home in Louisville, we chime in together, "I have no idea how we survived." (The Lord carried us, obviously.)

Mega Cat Fan

A poignant moment happened when my daddy was in his last hours. I can still picture Gordy kneeling by his bed, with one of his arms draped across Daddy's chest, praying for him.

It was about this desperate hour when my friend Jane (the fearless leader of the Abbies) arrived, bearing huge cups of her special iced tea. God bless her, and God bless those friends who appear out of nowhere with exactly what you didn't know you needed.

Daddy was a tough nut to crack. He could err on the impatient side on occasion (those of you who knew him are smiling). But deep down, he had a tender heart.

I'm a confessed Daddy's girl. He not only spoiled me, but what tickled and thrilled me most was how fascinated he was by our boys. We talked every day about the boys' antics, just like close friends enjoy doing. "What? You too?" He was a proficient balcony person.

A die-hard Kentucky Wildcat fan, Daddy's the only one I know who would schedule his hip replacement surgery around the Kentucky football schedule. When our boys decided to attend the University of Kentucky, no one could've been happier. (You can't exactly be born in Lexington, live down the street from Joe B. Hall, and not bleed blue. Some say Daddy brainwashed me, but I beg to differ.)

One gift I gave him, which I now love and cherish, is *The Life Application Bible*. After much prodding from myself and my mother, Daddy finally enrolled in Bible Study Fellowship. Mother was taking BSF in Lexington while I was taking it in Louisville.

You may recall the stubbornness with which I fought going to my first Bible study. Quadruple that, and you'll arrive at Daddy's determination to *not* attend anything of the sort. His standoff lasted until a brand-new church was built right across the street from their neighborhood. And guess what they were offering? Yes, a night-time, men's BSF class.

You can run, but you can't hide. No excuses left. God was clearly chasing down my father like nobody's business. Mother and I were in his balcony, cheering him on.

As I frequently flip through Daddy's Bible, his BSF notes still tucked in it, I love to see his handwriting. There's also a pamphlet in the Bible entitled "Steps to Assurance Regarding Your Relationship to Jesus Christ." Solid assurance for me that Daddy accepted Christ. Another gift from the Lord.

Bookworm

I suppose you could say my mother and I were friends; frenemies would be more like it. Kidding. Sorta. As we say in the South, "She could start an argument in an empty house."

We got along by arguing. Not sure who was more stubborn. My cousins and I call this stubbornness the "Daves factor." Mother was one of a slew of Daves kids. She and her siblings possessed this little trait. (Please don't ask my better half or my children if I'm blessed with it. I'm afraid to hear the answer.)

One common love of Mother's and mine was for our boys. As with Daddy, our best conversations centered around the boys. They provided us with multiple stories. Daily.

I also inherited my mother's love for reading. When Mother and Daddy lived in Owensboro before moving to Lexington, Mother was in a book club. I never knew that story until I began helping with the book club at Southeast. In addition to her own books, she was always on the hunt for good quality children's books. She gave our boys countless books.

Mother's death followed Daddy's seventeen months later. She may put me in time-out once I join her in heaven. She explicitly told me she did *not* want an open casket, but we had it open. (Forgive me, Mother, but I did it because you looked so pretty.) This time we were in her balcony, cheering her on to glory.

Inspiration to Go

Yes, well, I'd love to tell you to work on your shopping anointing, but I'd probably get in trouble for that one. (I can see my John rolling his eyes.) However, shopping with sister-friends and finding bargains together is victorious frolic. Maybe make a contest to see who can find the best bargain on your spree.

If you have a new baby in your family, start praying now for his or her spouse. It's never too early, and it won't cost you a penny.

Research experiences you can offer your loved ones (instead of giving them more things; we all have too much stuff). A trip somewhere, like Pam researches to take with her kids, is invaluable. Perhaps start a travel fund for your next adventure.

Endeavor to grow your relationships with friends from church or your Bible study groups. They'll feel like family in no time.

Look for ways to be in your loved ones' balconies. How can you cheer them on, on a regular basis? (Maybe add reminders to your calendar?)

As we move to our last stop, leaving family behind, you'll get a glimpse of those who feel like family. I dub them "practically kin." Unlike family, ahem, you can kinda choose or defect from your practically kin. (Don't quote me on that.)

Best BLT Sandwich

After telling you about making BLTs in Lisa Samson's kitchen on our very first stop, it just naturally flows for us to have a recipe for a good one. Comfort food to me. Try a couple of these little tricks to make the next BLT you create delight anyone who joins you:

Ingredients
White bread, toasted (your preference; pick whole wheat or multigrain, if you prefer)
Homegrown tomatoes, sliced
Duke's mayonnaise (if you can find it); dollop small amount into a bowl
Lettuce slices (again, your choice of greens)
Fresh basil, chopped and stirred into the mayonnaise
Avocados, sliced
Bacon

Directions
- Fry up some bacon, draining off the grease. Place on paper towel to absorb grease.
- Chop the basil, stirring into the mayonnaise. (Amounts vary depending upon how many sandwiches you're making and how much mayonnaise you like.)
- Spread basil mayonnaise onto both sides of your toast. On one side of the toast, add a slice or two of lettuce, tomatoes, avocado, and bacon. Close sandwich with other slice of toast. Enjoy.

Another version of this is to use guacamole as your spread. It makes the sandwich zestier, and you can still use slices of avocado, if you love avocados like I do.

Tenth Stop: Inviting
(Practically Kin)

A real conversation always contains an invitation. You
are inviting another person to reveal herself or himself
to you, to tell you who they are or what they want.[1]
—David Whyte

Fancy invitations fascinate this craft-impaired gal. The more
ornamentation, the better. I talked about Denise on our second
stop, and she deserves another shout-out in this chapter since it's all
about the shared activity of inviting. She all but gave me therapy in
choosing countless invitations. At the end of the day, we all want to
be invited, which translates into being included.

Sadly, this didn't occur to me in college. Thankfully, there was a special girl who befriended me back then. I learned firsthand how important it is to extend an invitation because when you're on the receiving end, there's nothing better. We'll see how this shakes out on this last stop.

Friendly Encounters

Like Marte and me, this sister-friend and I were also sorority sisters. "What? You too?" While she was a year younger, we frequently got to hang out in the Theta house and drop in on parties. We became adept at staying out and up late, which didn't mesh so well with our classes. How any of us nailed passing grades is a wonder.

Lisa Zaring is this special sister. We graduated, got married, and began having babies close to the same time, both living in Louisville.

In this season, several of our friends were also having babies. Lisa was running the Nanny Program at Sullivan College (now University). One of her jobs was placing nannies into homes on Fridays for their externships. Lisa was most gracious in gifting many of us with a nanny on Friday. (Translation: best friend ever.)

When Monday rolled around and you'd had zero sleep the entire weekend thanks to your newborn, you could totally hang on because you knew Friday was a-comin'.

Lisa's nannies would arrive bright and early on Friday morning. This dear nanny would tackle the laundry. Hallelujah.

She would feed the baby. Hallelujah *again*.

She would diaper the baby. Bigger hallelujah.

She would play with the baby so you could have a shower in peace and maybe even a nap. Gigantic hallelujah. (I'm just now realizing Lisa may have been the key to my sanity during those years.)

Now that our kids are grown, Lisa and I find time to meet for lunch and pick up wherever we last left off. We each try to treat each other to lunch, never remembering who bought the last time. We should probably let our server decide or fork out the bucks and try Focus Factor.

The point is, in the beginning, when I didn't think I could make it another sleepless night, Lisa thought to include me in her nanny program. Just knowing she thought about what I might need at that time made all the difference then. And now.

In Their Own Words

Just like Lisa, there are several others who showed me it only takes an invitation to cultivate sister-friends, whether it's from a serious scenario such has having a preemie or dealing with cancer; or with a visiting sibling; or from an inviting painting; or from our precious gospel.

It Only Takes an Invitation

Of all our friends who had babies together, Lisa remains the stalwart one. How she got through having her second child very prematurely, suddenly in labor at twenty-nine weeks and not being able to stop it, is still astonishing.

Patrick is her little miracle. He is one cool dude today. You'd never know he barely survived those first few weeks. We praise you, Lord.

Lisa may weep while reminiscing, but it was her faith and courage that kept us strong for her. God held her up. She just kept doing the next thing, taking the next step.

While you'd think we would've been her support, it worked the opposite way. I suppose because we had no idea what to do. Sometimes, the only thing a friend needs to do is just show up.

Walking alongside her was another uncomfortable yes because having a preemie is terrifying. I still cringe, wondering if our fears were written all over our faces. This was another blessed example of teamwork.

Let's hear from Lisa on the importance of an invitation:

When I consider why I'm drawn to certain people, it usually comes down to some sort of shared history or interest, or memory-making life event. These friendships are formed from a bond we've created, or, more realistically, they're a God-orchestrated match.

The Maker of all things both great and small does realize where we are and what we need at all times. When we look back at how our friendships have evolved, we can see the many ties we've made. We come away amazed and thankful: high school, college, marriage, babies, clubs, Bible studies, church, and work. These are the ties that bind.

These friends rallied by my side over the years. When we were finally able to bring Patrick home after his way-too-early arrival, a bundle of yellow balloons was left tied to our front steps. Numerous, fervent prayers were sent up. Meals were delivered to help our transition from hospital to home. Cute poems were written to lighten the mood, and my friends kept showing up in many different ways. Praise God for miracles.

While the Lord helped us over the hurdle with Patrick, another detour was around the next turn: divorce.

Divorce can wreck you deep to your core, but oh, how your friends can lift you up. My friends continued to invite me in, check on me, pray *with* me and *for* me, never giving up on me—even when I had very little to give in return. These are the ties that bind.

Celebrations allow us to share happy times, but it doesn't have to be a big event that ties us together. Any small gesture can have a huge impact when delivered from a friend who knows you well. A quick lunch date, a telephone call, a walking partner, a card sent with care and concern, an invitation. These are the ties that bind.

It's the *invitation* that's most important to me. One that says, "I'm here for you. I'm with you. I want you to be included. I want to share the good news."

These are two of my favorite verses on these ties that bind:

"Two are better than one; because they have good reward for their labor. For if they fall, the one will lift up his fellow; but woe to him that is alone when he falleth; for he hath not another to help him up" (Ecclesiastes 4:9–10 KJV) and "Beyond all these things put on love, which is the perfect bond of unity" (Colossians 4:13 NASB).

Lisa is still at it today. Whether it's lunch with the girls or dinner that includes our husbands, she's always thinking of how to involve others. She's inspired me to look for people who might need to be included, lifted up, or just smiled at. (Sidebar: Only because I love Lisa do I allow her and her beautiful firstborn, Elizabeth, to call me "Big Elizabeth." Mercy.)

Next up is a darling young friend of mine who happens to be a Butter Babe-in-Training. Even though she's now thirty-something, she's still considered in training because she's one of the Butter Babes' daughters. Hey, respect your elders.

Sibling Separation Solved with an Invitation

This Butter Babe-in-Training is Becky Aguiar Jarrell. She and her adorable son, Silas, live in Atlanta. You met her hilarious Butter Babe mom, Nancy the Hugging Evangelist, on our fourth stop. Becky landed in this chapter since she's practically kin.

When Becky was leaving for college, her little brother, Scotty, didn't take to her departure very well. He slipped a note under the bathroom door for Becky, an invitation, if you will, to take his two dollars with her to college should she need it. At the time, that kind of sacrifice bonded these two all the more:

> I have friends who I tell my deepest, darkest secrets to about motherhood and everyday stress, but with my brother, I don't have to say any of that. He already knows. He can read it on my face, and he can hear my heartache through texts and emails like only a brother could.
>
> He calls at exactly the right moments with the perfect words to say on the worst day of my year. And he can send me a funny picture on my best day of the week. It makes me all the happier. Though four hundred miles separate us physically, emotionally, I know he's with me always.

I know hearing Becky's affections for Scotty warms her parents' hearts. Isn't that what we as parents pray for, for our own children? Becky and Scotty are in each other's balconies, cheering each other on, as we learned about on our last stop. No sibling rivalry there. And now, invitations from Becky to visit Atlanta delight her entire family. They jump at an opportunity for a road trip.

Inviting Prayer In

Yet one more Babe-in-Training, affectionately known as "Lil' Bit," is Sarah Grace Bloyd. She's the daughter of Faithful Fay, another Butter Babe.

Born prematurely, Sarah Grace jumped miraculous hurdles and graduated early from college. She hangs with the rest of us, sharing new tidbits we never knew existed. Our only-child upbringings have allowed us numerous, "What? You too?" moments. Precisely why I feel like she, too, is practically kin.

Let's hear about her little experiment with John 15:13: "There is no greater love than to lay down one's life for one's friends" (NLT). Notice she invites the Lord to show her what friendship really looks like in different scenarios.

Each time I heard the verse, John 15:13 ("The greatest love you can show is to give your life for your friends"), I drew back a little in disbelief, wanting to say, "Hold the phone, Jesus. You're telling me the greatest kind of love happens when someone is willing to *die* for his or her friends? I mean, it's a lovely sentiment, but throughout most of my life, I've had friends that check out, burn out, and flake out faster than I do at the end of a semester." It would be safe to assume a commitment like that didn't exactly fit into my idea of friendship at the time.

Eventually, I got so fed up with it all, I decided to go back to the source, Jesus, to see what kind of groundwork needed to be in place for those all-or-nothing friendships to take root. If Jesus said it, He must have known what it took to have friends who were worth everything.

Jesus is the best model of a life-laid-down kind of friend. He laughed with His friends, cried with them, got sassy with them, advised them, and served them, but most importantly, He prayed for them. Prayer. *That* was the missing piece.

Surely taking my friendships straight to the throne of grace would be a game changer, inviting Him to show me His way of befriending.

> When my friends were celebrating, I asked Jesus to multiply my joy to pour out on them. When they were hurting, I asked Him to break my heart right along with theirs. When they needed advice, my request of the Father was for equal parts of grace and truth to take shape.
>
> Suddenly, this group of people I call friends I thought had just been thrown together had actually been orchestrated by the Creator to make an eternal difference. They aren't just in my life to pass the time. They really are friends worth dying for.

Yes! Bravo for Sarah Grace working through her own uncomfortable yes. Between the Lord and His Word, Sarah Grace was challenged to model her friendships right after Him.

Ministering with Cancer

Thanks to Christian Academy of Louisville, where our kids went to school, the book club, and a few Bible studies, I was blessed to become acquainted with a beautiful young woman named Denita Arnold. She even shared her powerful testimony at one of our book club meetings one evening.

Denita's sister, Asia, founded A Woman Like You Foundation, which helps women facing the challenges of their cancer journey. After Asia went to be with the Lord, Denita picked up the ball and is now the president of this organization. We would all say that's a club we wouldn't want to be a part of, but hey, if you have cancer, wouldn't you want to be *invited* in to receive help?

Run and fetch a Kleenex, as you'll need it when you hear Denita tell of her precious relationship with her sister:

It was Saturday morning when I arrived at the hospital. We'd just been there the night before. This was now part of our routine.

I walked down the long hallway, opening the door. There she lay. Quiet. Still. My heart sank. Was I too late? In slow motion, I walked up to her bed and touched her.

"Sister?" I whispered.

In one quiet in-and-out sigh, she replied, "Hey, Sister." I loved it when she called me that. I fought back tears of relief, realizing we still had more time.

I knew I had to make the dreaded calls. "Come quickly. I'm not sure how much longer she can hold on."

As I waited for the others to arrive, I slid into the bed with her and held her hand. "Don't go to sleep, Sister," I said. "Everyone's on their way to see you. Let's sing."

"Okay," she agreed. "What should we sing?"

I began to sing, "Jesus loves me this I know, for the Bible tells me so. Little ones to Him belong, they are weak but He is strong. Yes, Jesus loves me ... The Bible tells me so."

She chimed in, laboring to get the words out while reminding me with a small chuckle, "You know you can't sing, right?"

"Yes, I know. But let's sing it again anyway," I pleaded.

And so it was, the beginning of the end we knew would soon come. My mind raced back with infinite thoughts of our past, present, and future. It was just yesterday we were three little girls running around outside, playing from dawn to dusk. It was just yesterday we were teenagers arguing over clothes and room space. It was just yesterday we were young women dreaming about our future.

A common phrase I used to describe my admiration of her was, "When I grow up, I want to be just like her." Innocent, kind, smart, beautiful, lover of Jesus. We had grown from the dynamics of sisters to the privilege of friends.

"Sister," she said, "You've been taking care of me since we were young. Thank you."

This was a blessing to hear. It made up for the times I'd shut her out or left her behind, the times I retreated into my own life and thought more of myself than others. Still, she remembered what was important.

Regrets evaporated. Only love remained. I was there every step of the way, as we battled the cancer together.

God would give us just the amount of days we needed. Not one went wasted. She wouldn't let it. She reminded every nurse, doctor, worker, family member, and visitor how much they were loved. Loved by her, but most of all loved by Jesus. It was the way she'd learned to live each day. Evermore grateful, knowing the outcome. Lying in a hospital bed didn't change her attitude in her remaining days.

"Do you know how much Jesus loves you?" she would ask. "You are special, and God has big plans for you! My life is ending, but *you* can still do something with yours. I love you." On and on she went, inviting anyone who entered her room to become acquainted with her Lord and Savior. Hugs, laughter, songs, prayer, and even photos transpired with her contagious smile.

As the days went by, she began slipping in and out of the arms of Jesus. She was ready, but we were not.

> Once again, I slipped into her bed. My second feeble attempt to comfort her with song was met with her eyes closed and tears streaming down her cheeks. We held her hands, my mom, our other sister, Venus, and me.
>
> Mom left. In the quiet of the room, it was just us three sisters alone. Venus and I chattered softly into the darkness of the night, laughing quietly while reminiscing.
>
> Suddenly, Venus asked, "Do you hear that?"
>
> And in a moment, which was all too sudden, nothing. No sound. No movement. No breath. Only a sweet smile to say, "I've arrived, and I am safe in His arms."
>
> It was the saddest day of our lives, but the best day for Asia.
>
> We love her. We miss her. We celebrate her. We will see her again.
>
> Our sister, our friend.

Losing a sibling at such a young age seems unnatural. In Denita's case, the legacy her sister left, as well as the foundation she started, is supporting others who are battling cancer. This is a huge case for making your misery your ministry, inviting others in.

The more natural progression seems to be when our parents travel heavenward. Many of my friends are in the season of losing their parents. The aging process, as we all know, is inevitable, and while we pray our parents into heaven, their journey in getting there can be daunting and difficult.

An Inviting Painting and a Momma's Heart

Alzheimer's has plagued several of my friends' parents. Recently, two of them lost their mothers to this challenging disease.

My friend Jayne (the Ya-Yas' calendar coordinator) and I

attended the funeral of my friend Sherry's mother. It was lovely in every way, celebrating Sherry's mother's life. In many ways, I feel like the funeral somewhat prepared us for what Jayne would soon be going through with her own mother.

I recently ran across the program from Jayne's mother's funeral. I kept it because I loved the colorful, tranquil painting on the cover. It's of a man in tuxedo tails, complete with a brilliant white handkerchief in his pocket. He seems to be dancing. One leg is kicked out, and both arms are extended, as if the top of the letter "A." A full harvest moon is behind him, while stars are twinkling in the clouds over him. A winged cherub is swinging a floral garland over this dancing man.

The quote underneath reads, "When I get to heaven and I'm all settled there, may I dine with Mr. Disney ... and dance with Fred Astaire?" Artist D. Morgan painted the picture and wrote the quote.

I'm not sure what made me keep it, but several months after the funeral, I ran across it again and called Jayne to find out if there was a story to the picture. She confirmed there is indeed a story, full of memories.

When Jayne was growing up, and *The Wonderful World of Disney* was on TV, Jayne's mother, Mary Jo, would pop popcorn for her three daughters. Jayne said it was a big deal for them to get to stay up and watch the show, munching on popcorn in their PJs, all together. What a sweet memory.

Jayne's mom was a big fan of both Walt Disney and Fred Astaire. She was delighted to find D. Morgan's painting with the quote and immediately had it framed. It hung in her room as long as Jayne can remember. Jayne thought it'd be appropriate to be on the cover of the program for her mother's funeral. Mary Jo must be so very proud of Jayne.

This past Christmas, I connected with the artist, landing six copies of this painting for all the Ya-Yas. It's not only symbolic of our life-giving friendships, the painting in many ways invites us in to savor memories of our parents as well as our time dancing together at our children's weddings.

Pastor Rick Warren reminds us of our spiritual family: "God's family is going to outlast even your physical family. Physical families don't last. They grow up, they move away, they die. But the spiritual family of God is going to go on and on for eternity."[2]

My sister-in-love Marte gifted me with a comforting thought when we were talking after both losing our parents. She said, "I'm just glad we're only shortly separated."

As we live with an eternal perspective, God is greatly pleased when we diligently plant seeds of the gospel while still here on earth. This translates into extending an invitation into the Kingdom. Don't we all aspire to take as many people with us as we can to heaven?

In good times and bad, this must be on the forefront of our minds. Jamie Marshall Dorr is a darling young gal who's very close friends with our kiddos. She and her husband, Jake, live in Mississippi, but they get back to Louisville to see family and friends as often as they can. We claim them as practically kin.

They recently had a beautiful baby boy, named Barron Jacob Dorr. For some unknown reason, Barron was never able to breathe on his own. Thousands of us prayed for him in countless ways, for the doctors, for his test results, for comfort for all three of them, and so on. Sadly, two months after Barron was born, he landed in the arms of Jesus.

The doctors declared he died of an "unexplainable" neurological condition. The very next day, Jamie said she and Jake would miss Barron every single second of every single day. Then she boldly declared:

> For now, Mama's got work to do. She has to tell as many people about Jesus that she can so that the Kingdom increases. We live in a world that needs Jesus. And so, even through all of this excruciating pain, this is what I know: God is still on the throne. He has never failed us and never will. God, the creator of the universe, is who He says He is. This separation isn't finite. We will see each other again.

If Jamie, a young mom, having just lost her son, can declare God's goodness and glory, inviting as many people as she can into the Kingdom, why can't we?

"But," you may be saying, "I'm not qualified to share the gospel with a stranger or friend or family member."

I've got a simple solution for you, straight from my dear friend and pastor, Bob Russell.

The Gospel in One-Syllable Words: Another Simple Invitation

Bob tells of a time when he and his son, Rusty, had an opportunity to hear Dr. Lewis Foster speak. At the time, Rusty was only five years old. Dr. Foster was a New Testament professor at Cincinnati Christian University. He'd graduated from Yale and Harvard with honors and served on the translation team for the NIV Study Bible.

Bob says, "Dr. Foster is brilliant and gifted in communicating profound truth in exciting and understandable ways."

Rusty sorta sucker-punched Bob after they heard Dr. Foster speak by suggesting Bob try preaching like him because he could understand him.

Convicted, Bob said he determined to keep the message simple. "The power is in the gospel, *not* in our being clever with it," he added. So he sat down and wrote out the gospel in one-syllable words:

> God made man and loved him.
> Man sinned and fell from God's grace.
> But God, in His great love, sent His Son to die in our place, and then He raised him from the dead.
> Now if we put our faith in Him, He will cleanse our sins and give us life.

Sister-friend, tomorrow's not promised. If the Lord is tugging at your heart over a loved one or an acquaintance, go to them *now* and assure them you want them in heaven with you. Even if this is a big uncomfortable yes for you, invite them in and share the Good News.

Fear not… the Holy Spirit will equip.

Inspiration to Go

Extend an invitation to a friend. It doesn't have to be big-deal-extravagant, nor a printed paper one. Verbal is grand. Simply create an opportunity to catch up and spend time together, making them feel special from the invitation.

President Lincoln said, "The better part of one's life consists of his friendships." Invitations to spend time together will enhance your friendship.

Be bold, clear, and courageous, inviting those you're with to share your faith in easy, simple ways, as Bob suggests.

Keep eternity in your hearts. C. S. Lewis offers a great shout to all of us on our road to eternity: "Besides—Christians *never* say goodbye!"[3]

Sweet sister-friend, it's been sheer joy road-trippin' with you at our different stops, sharing my friends, our escapades, their words. I pray you've gathered some ideas of fun things to do with your friends and that y'all will cook up some of these melt-in-your-mouth recipes in this book, plus try the rest of 'em on my website (www.elizabethhoagland.com).

God's blessings to you and your family.

I'd love to hear stories from you about *you* and *your* sister-friends! Feel free to contact me at www.elizabethhoagland.com, or I'm on Facebook and Instagram (which causes our children to LOL).

Until we meet again…

Lemon Apricot Cake
(from Thelma Button)

Yes, well, I'm realizing there are *ten* recipes with chocolate in them (!!!) in our collection, so I thought a non-chocolate cake, while still delish, could be equally rewarding. Besides, this cake is easy, and everyone loves it, whether for after dinner or for brunch.

I learned of this recipe in my working days at Citizens Fidelity Bank. We had a darling teller who worked in our branch at the time named Jan Button. Well named, she was and still is cute as a button. Her mother, Thelma, invited our crew to come for dinner at Christmas time. Their home is beautiful and the whole evening was magical.

This recipe is for the cake she served. I was so taken aback by how delicious it was, surprising in many ways. I was more excited to learn I could reproduce it, pleasing many guests who later came our way.

Ingredients
Cake
    1 box Duncan Hines Lemon Supreme Cake Mix
    1 small box lemon Jello
    ¾ cup vegetable oil
    1 teaspoon lemon flavoring
    5 eggs
    1 cup of apricot nectar

Icing
    1 cup confectioner's sugar
    Juice from 1 or 2 lemons, to taste
    Dash of salt

Cake Directions
- Grease a Bundt cake pan.

- Throw all ingredients into a large mixing bowl. Beat for five minutes on high speed.
- Pour into pan and bake at 325 degrees for one hour.
- Set out on a cooling rack.
- Remove cake onto a platter. Drizzle with icing. Slice when ready.

Icing Directions
- While cake is cooling, mix together 1 cup of confectioner's sugar, lemon juice, and a dash of salt.

Homemade Fudge Cake and Chocolate Sauce
(from Meredith Myers)

When I was in second grade, we moved to a new home in Lexington. I discovered I was blessed with an across-the-street neighbor named Meredith. She was a year younger than I was and had not one, but two older brothers. Life was grand.

Not only was her mother a great cook, her grandmother was too. They called her grandmother, "Mom." Seems confusing now, but I never thought a thing about it growing up.

Mom and Meredith's mom (oh, we're having fun now!) made fudge cake and chocolate sauce on a regular basis. Depending on how many children were in the house, they would draw a line in the mixing bowl, giving us each rubber spatulas, and we could lick up our "section." I quickly learned to pray Meredith's brothers would be *away* for a scouting or sports event. That meant more batter to lick (selfish little second grader).

Meredith and I no longer live across the street from each other. Meredith, aka Madge (just to throw you one more name) lives in Nashville. We try to meet up here in Louisville or there in Nashville as often as we can.

Meredith is an angel to share these heavenly recipes. Aptly described, as both her mother and grandmother are with the Lord. She gives tips for us cooks along the way:

Ingredients
Mom's Fudge Cake
2 sticks butter (The recipe is so old, it says "oleo.")
2 cups sugar
4 eggs
4 squares bitter (unsweetened baking) chocolate (4 oz. total)
1⅓ cup flour
Dash of salt
3 teaspoons pure vanilla extract

Chopped pecans or chocolate chips for the top (optional)

Mom's Chocolate Sauce
    1 square unsweetened baking/bitter chocolate (1 oz.)

    1 scoop sugar (Meredith uses 1 cup.)

    ⅓ cup water

    ½ cup milk

    12–15 large marshmallows

    Dash of salt

    1–2 teaspoons pure vanilla extract

Directions
Fudge Cake

- Preheat oven to 325 degrees.
- Grease two 7 x 11 pans (Meredith says they called them fudge cake pans; you can also use an 11 × 13 size) She actually lines them with wax paper like her grandmother did.
- Melt butter and chocolate on stove over low heat; stir until smooth; remove from heat and allow to cool slightly.
- In a bowl, lightly fork-beat the eggs. Add sugar, vanilla, flour, and salt and stir until blended.
- Add the chocolate/butter mixture to the egg/sugar/flour mixture. (Meredith says, "Mom always stirred some of the egg/sugar/flour mixture into the pan with the melted chocolate /butter first—to cool the chocolate so you don't scramble the eggs.")
- Pour batter into the pans; top with chocolate chips or chopped pecans to cover the top, if desired.
- Bake for about 25 minutes, until set. (They are too fudgy for the toothpick test.)
- Allow to cool 10–15 minutes in the pans. If you lined the pans with wax paper, turn them out onto a cutting board, peel the paper off, then cut into squares.
- Sprinkle tops with sifted powdered sugar.

Freezes well.

Chocolate Sauce

- Place first three ingredients in saucepan over low heat; allow to come to a boil and stir for about 5 minutes.
- Add milk slowly and let mixture return to a boil.
- Add marshmallows, stirring until melted.
- Remove from heat and stir in salt and vanilla extract.
- Serve warm. Great on fudge cake or ice cream.
- Refrigerate leftovers. It will firm up when cold, but reheats in the microwave or on stovetop.

Favorite Books from Past Book Club Meetings

(Listed Alphabetically by Author)

Tessa Afshar, *Pearl in the Sand*

Robert Bugh, *When the Bottom Drops Out: Finding Grace in the Depths of Disappointment*

Katie Davis, *Kisses from Katie: A Story of Relentless Love and Redemption*

Linda Dillow, *Calm My Anxious Heart: A Woman's Guide to Finding Contentment*

Chris Fabry, *Dogwood* and *The Promise of Jesse Woods*

Margaret Feinberg, *Scouting the Divine: My Search for God in Wine, Wool, and Wild Honey* and *Sacred Echo*

Ann Gabhart, *The Outsider* and *These Healing Hills*

Robin Jones Gunn, *Gardenias for Breakfast*

Ron Hall and Denver Moore, *Same Kind of Different as Me: A Modern-Day Slave, an International Art Dealer, and the Unlikely Woman Who Bound Them Together*

Liz Curtis Higgs, *A Wreath of Snow; Embrace Grace: Welcome to the Forgiven Life;* and *Thorn in My Heart* (We all loved *all* of the series set in Scotland.)

Angela Hunt, *The Note*

Karen Kingsbury, *The Redemption Series*

Max Lucado, *Traveling Light: Releasing the Burdens You Were Never Intended to Bear*

Sarah Mackenzie, *The Read-Aloud Family: Making Meaningful and Lasting Connections with Your Kids*

Charles Martin, *When Crickets Cry*

Lucinda Secrest McDowell, *Quilts from Heaven: Parables from the Patchwork of Life; Refresh! A Spa for Your Soul;* and *Ordinary Graces: Word Gifts for Every Season*

Eric Metaxas, *Miracles: What They Are, Why They Happen, and How They Can Change Your Life*

Robert J. Morgan, *The Promise: God Works All Things Together for Your Good; The Lord Is My Shepherd: Resting in the Peace and Power of Palm 23;* and *The Red Sea Rules: 10 God-Given Strategies for Difficult Times*

Anita Renfroe, *The Purse-Driven Life: It Really Is All about Me*

Francine Rivers, *Redeeming Love*

Erin Smalley and Carrie Oliver, *Grown-Up Girlfriends: Finding Real Friends in the Real World*

Hannah Whitall Smith, *The Christian's Secret for a Happy Life*

Ken Tada and Joni Eareckson Tada, *Joni and Ken: An Untold Love Story*

Lysa TerKeurst, *The Best Yes: Making Wise Decisions in the Midst of Endless Demands*

John Trent and Gary Smalley, *The Blessing: Giving the Gift of Unconditional Love and Acceptance*

Michelle Ule, *Mrs. Oswald Chambers: The Woman behind the World's Bestselling Devotional* and *A Poppy in Remembrance*

Sheldon Vanauken, *A Severe Mercy*

Ann Voskamp, *One Thousand Gifts: A Dare to Live Fully Right Where You Are*

Discussion Questions for Book Clubs or Small Groups

When helping with a book club years ago, we were hugely relieved if our selection had discussion questions (otherwise, we had to come up with our own, which were sketchy at best). I pray the below questions bring forth grand discussions for you in your small group or book club. May they give you more to think about for yourself and your friends, elevating your friendships.

1. Name a couple of your favorite books. What traits do those books have in common that make them so good? The book clubs I've been a part of made a concerted effort to offer a variety of selections. Some I wouldn't have known about, had we not read them. Do you prefer fiction or nonfiction? Which book would you recommend to a friend or perhaps to a book club you attend? Would you consider starting a book club if you're not part of one?

2. Author Bob Merritt parallels his wife's spaghetti and meatballs to friendship, dubbing his close friends "meatball friends." He says as his wife's meatballs simmer all day with the sauce, they become part of the sauce, as does the sauce become part of the meatballs. He adds, "When it comes to friends, it's the quality of the meat and the quantity of the heat.... Once you find quality friends, you need to add heat and simmer time."[1]

   My Ya-Yas are definitely my meatball friends (don't miss the recipe Kathy and Matthew gifted us with at the end of the Sixth Stop). We've had fantastic simmer time. Who are your meatball friends? What does adding heat look like in a friendship? What about simmer time?

3. Cakes and other fun foods play an integral role with my Bible study buddies. The shallow side of my Abbies and B on B girls surface because we're so easily enticed to attend Bible study when food is on the table. How about you and your friends? Do you have a favorite restaurant where you meet or a favorite dish one of you makes to share? What are they, and would you share the recipe?

4. When we met the Butter Babes on our fourth stop, I told of the time Fay organized a number of women and a bountiful amount of food for a meal after my mother's funeral. I confessed I was challenged to accept all the help and generosity they brought with them. (I'd have much rather been on the serving end versus the receiving end.) How well do you receive things from your friends? How can you focus on your friends' thoughtfulness, perhaps their motivation, as opposed to worrying how you'll put that gift to use?

5. Each one of the friends I talk about on our fifth stop brings accountability and intentionality to the friendship table. They keep me on my toes. Who does that for you? And who do you keep on their toes? What does that look like?

6. One of many enviable traits my Elizabethan Sisters from our sixth stop possess is they are both incredibly flexible. Not much of anything ruffles their feathers. Claude Chabrol describes them perfectly: "You have to accept that sometimes you're the pigeon, and sometimes you're the statue."[2] How flexible are you? How about your friends? What's one way you could perhaps add some flexibility to your calendar and your friendships?

7. Praying with my prayer warriors has been educational, to say the least. We've learned to ask intentionally and specifically regarding our concerns. Becky taught us boldness and determination. If

you've been in a prayer group for a while, what have you learned about a praying life? If you're not yet in a prayer group, what would it take for you to start one?

8. Being a prayer warrior, especially for a prodigal, requires hard work. From your own experience, how have you experienced the Lord at work in the life of a prodigal? Are you a journaler? If not, were you inspired by Olivia Mitchell's prodding per her mother's journal on our eighth stop? What changes in your prayer life will you implement this week?

9. As our journey together is ending, we're still ultimately heading heavenward. Therefore, we still need to keep an eternal perspective. Pam's idea does just that; she has dumped gift-giving for birthdays, as in things (which you can't take with you to heaven), and has embraced the giving of experiences to each of her children, one on one, exploring and learning about new places. What kind of experience would you like to give to a family member or a friend? Do you have a place you like to return to time after time, or do you want to go somewhere new? Where would that be? And where would that be if money were no object?

10. Our last stop explores the invitation—the joy of being invited, being included. What are some ways you could invite someone for a quick cup of coffee? Can you think of someone you'd like to know better or who perhaps needs your ear? Can you think of someone who needs to hear the gospel? Pray about who you can invite into the Kingdom.

Discussion Questions for Bible Study

These questions have been written for you and your sister-friends who'd like to do a Bible study together. Whether you're taking ten weeks, or five, or however you slice it to complete this study, I pray these questions help you search scripture and your soul for the answers. May you be honest ("Before a word is on my tongue, you, LORD, know it completely": Psalm 139:4), bold, and blessed by your study in finding answers and by hearing each other's answers.

As we've journeyed along together on our ten different stops, may these questions (and answers) be your passport, equipping you heavenward. May they go from your head, to your heart, all the way down to your toes, your feet now walking where the rubber meets the road.

You may wish to grab a notepad or a journal to write down your answers (unless you prefer writing in the margins).

First Stop: Discovering (Friends from Book Club)

1. Attending a book club is great fun. You make friends and get to read a variety of books, food almost always factors into the equation, and learning from discussions, well, what more could you ask for? Behind the scenes, however, many of us were often puzzled over choosing which books to read. We arrived at

Christian fiction and nonfiction by reading reviews and praying over the sometimes forty-five books, for only nine slots.

a. What eight attributes does Philippians 4:8 include? How could you apply this as a filter for what you read and watch at the movies or on TV? I once heard Zig Ziglar say, "Get rid of the G-I-G-O." He explained, "Garbage in, garbage out." Ick. Let's reread Philippians 4:8 together: "Finally, brothers and sisters, whatever is true, whatever is noble, whatever is right, whatever is pure, whatever is lovely, whatever is admirable—if anything is excellent or praiseworthy—think about such things."

b. To add to those attributes above, write down the seven attributes of heavenly wisdom found in James 3:17.

2. Discussion in our book club meetings was always rich and full of pearls to take home. Women of all ages offered advice, experiences, even additional book recommendations (because for sure we all need *more* books).

a. What are we to strive for, according to 2 Corinthians 13:11? How can we encourage one another? What's the result?

b. Ephesians 4:2–6 includes the phrase "unity of the Spirit." How many instructions do you find in this passage? How are you encouraged by this?

3. Whether it's words spoken or written, we all love positive remarks. Sadly, sometimes it's easier to recall the negative versus the positive. How are kind words and timely advice described in Proverbs 16:24: ("Kind words are like honey—sweet to the soul and healthy for the body" and Proverbs 25:11 ("Timely advice is lovely, like golden apples in a silver basket" (NLT)? What are the benefits? Think of someone who needs encouraging and jot them a quick note this week.

Second Stop: Life-Giving (Friends Thanks to Our Kids: The Ya-Yas)

1. As the Ya-Yas recently had their silver anniversary, I've realized many topics we discuss are universal in all friendships. Since death and disease have touched all our lives (starting out on a cheery note, aren't we?), we'll start with mourning and then happily progress toward tender togetherness.

    a. Let's begin with Ecclesiastes 3:4. What four activities are in this verse? Which of these have you and your friends done together? Which of these four is your favorite?

    b. Look at Romans 12:15. What are we supposed to do? What would you deem the key word to be in these two phrases? What's the benefit? Read through Isaiah 35:10. What five fabulous things will happen to our loved ones who've gone ahead of us?

    c. Not only are we blessed to have friends to journey these rough roads with us, peek at Psalm 18:32 and see what our Almighty God does for us.

2. Thanks to our cell phones, the phone companies are bemoaning the good ol' days of high long-distance bills. The Ya-Yas keep their phones pretty well lit, minutes of conversation often morphing into hours. When we can miraculously steal away for an overnight gathering, we fall asleep sitting up, talking.

    a. Obviously, finding something to talk about is never a challenge for the Ya-Yas. Best-case scenario is found in Proverbs 15:23. What do we see about our replies?

    b. Worst-case scenario is found in Proverbs 17:9, from the Contemporary English Version: "You will keep your friends if you forgive them, but you will lose your friends if you keep talking about what they did wrong." What does this mean to you? Have you seen such a scenario play out before?

c. Unbelievably, Kathy spoke at Joe's funeral. She, along with the rest of the speakers, exemplified Galatians 6:14: "But it's *unthinkable* that I could ever brag about *anything* except the cross of our Lord Jesus Christ. By his cross my relationship to the world and its relationship to me have been crucified" (God's Word Translation, emphasis mine). Do you find it easy or challenging to boast about the Lord? Would you say you're bold about your faith or timid? Think about a God-honoring phrase you could interject into your next conversation with a stranger or a friend. Share this with your group.

3. Face-to-face time together with friends is the best, when possible. First, we'll look at a definition of friendship, and then we'll see why friends are so important.
   a. In Proverbs 17:17, what does a friend do and what are our sisters (same as "brother" in the passage) to do?
   b. Why are we better off with a friend than being alone, per Ecclesiastes 4:9–10? How would you put this verse into your own words?

Third Stop: Understanding (Friends from Bible Study)

1. The Abbies and the B on B gals tote spiritual fruit home from our Bible study meetings each week. This experience yields many benefits. This week, we'll start shallow, as in "What should I wear?" and move to why it's so important to fill our minds with God's Word, wisdom, and teaching.
   a. What snare do we need to beware of in Proverbs 29:25? Do any of you suffer from the disease to please? How do you avoid it? What must we do, according to this verse, to be kept safe?
   b. Worrying about what we wear could also fit into that "disease to please" category. What are we to clothe ourselves

with in Colossians 3:12–14? Why are we to bear with each other? What's the outcome of this new wardrobe?

2. Now let's look at how God's Word is described and what we can learn from it.
   a. Look up Proverbs 30:5. (Note it says *"every"* word, not "some" words.) What is *every* word? What does that mean to you? What piece of armor does the Lord represent? What comfort do you gain from this verse?
   b. What additional benefits do we gain from Proverbs 6:23? Why was all this written, according to Romans 15:4? What's the result?
   c. What example does Ezra set for us in Ezra 7:10? How does the Lord equip us in Proverbs 2:6?

3. Regarding how the Abbies got their name, we discovered it's because we often feel like foreigners in another land. Going against the crazy culture of today is not always easy.
   a. What instruction does Romans 12:2 offer? What is the result?
   b. What does Colossians 3:1–3 add to that instruction?
   c. While we're not clear on who authored Psalm 119, some speculate Ezra, which would be cool, given his example we read in Ezra 7. First, look at verses 15–18 from Psalm 119. How would you describe these phrases: "meditate on your precepts," "consider your ways," and "delight in your decrees"? How does he conclude verse 16? What prayerful request is in verse 18? As a group, take verses 169–176 and discuss each verse, looking at what its request is and what the result is. Let's read together a goal for us students from the Living Bible in 2 Peter 3:18: "But grow in spiritual strength and become better acquainted with our Lord and Savior Jesus Christ. To him be all glory and splendid honor,

both now and forevermore. Goodbye." (Yes, it really says, "Goodbye"!)

Fourth Stop: Laughing (Friends from Butter: The Butter Babes)

1. I love, love, L-O-V-E my Butter Babes. I love *all* my friends, for that matter, but I decided we should look at some verses on love to see how God's Word spells this out. As we're analyzing this, keep your own friends in mind and be thinking how you can show love toward them.

    "Love" is all over the Bible; we could spend nearly two years reading a verse a day on love, so this week, let's just look at three:

    a. Look up 1 Peter 4:8–10. First, what does love *do*? And then what are *we* to do?

    b. Now go to Ephesians 3:16–18. What does the Holy Spirit do for us and why? What do we receive if we're rooted and established in love? (Note that we are *not* alone in this.)

    c. What does 1 Samuel 18:1 tell us about David and Jonathan? Do you have friendships like this? Can you describe what that feels like?

2. Now let's talk about joy. The Butter Babes ooze with joy. They bring me joy. They make me feel joyful. When we get together, we're all better off when we leave each other than when we first arrived. Can you think of some of your joy-filled friends? How do they bring you joy?

    a. Look up Jeremiah 31:3–4. How does the Lord love us? Which two, two-word phrases does He use to bring us comfort? What promises does He give us? Have you donned your dancin' shoes?

    b. Look up Nehemiah 8:10. What are the marching papers Nehemiah issues? What kind of day is it? What is our strength?

c.   What is being made known to us in Psalm 16:11? With what are we filled, and who's with us? Is this temporary?

3.   Nobody likes stale anything. We like things *fresh*. Fresh fruit, fresh vegetables, fresh chocolate (gotcha). Even better, when you're tired or down in the dumps, don't you want to be refreshed? Let's find out where we can be refreshed.

   a.   Look up Philemon 7. Paul is writing his dear friend Philemon. What two things does he say Philemon's love gave him? And what did Philemon do to the hearts of the Lord's people?

   b.   What's the outcome in Romans 15:32 when Paul asks his brothers and sisters in Christ to pray for him as he plans to go to Rome? In what two ways will he come to them, and what will he experience from them? What's an example of being refreshed by others today?

   c.   Proverbs 27:9b says, "A sweet friendship refreshes the soul" (The Message). Jot down the name of a friend you can in some way refresh this week.

4.   We talked about laughter being good medicine with the Butter Babes, or any friendship, for that matter. Laughter has *many* health benefits; therefore, the Babes keep me healthy (perfectly logical equation). Let's look at a few verses to encourage us to hunt down laughter with our friends:

   a.   What is Proverbs 31:25 telling us about the future? Do you wear what this Proverbs 31 woman wears? Who comes to mind when you think of someone "clothed with strength and dignity"?

   b.   Psalm 126:2 blesses us with laughter, song, and praise. Which phrases align with these three activities?

   c.   Butter Babe Nancy (the Hugging Evangelist) makes us howl with laughter when she keeps saying, "I am the worst" (she refers to 1 Timothy 1:15–17). While this is a serious verse, it's a beautiful reminder for us. Paul declares God's mercy on us to be "trustworthy, deserving full acceptance." Why does he say Jesus came? What does the Lord show us, and then best of all, what does He display for each of us?

Fifth Stop: Soul-Stretching (Friends from Walking)

1. My walking buddies not only help me get a little exercise out of the way, they fine-tune whatever's happenin' in my corner of the world. On our fifth stop, we talked about iron sharpening iron. My friends' encouragement to keep our feet headed in the right direction has been invaluable.
   a. Let's first look at who walked with God in the Bible. Look up Genesis 5:22–24, 6:9, and 17:1. List the names of these men who walked with God. What was an attribute they all shared?
   b. What does 2 John 6 label as walking in obedience? In the English Standard Version, look up Leviticus 18:4–5. Is walking in statutes the same idea John is talking about in the previous verse? What does this look like in our everyday lives?
   c. What do we receive when we walk in the light of the Lord's presence, according to Psalm 89:15? Picking up the pace from walking to jogging, what race does Hebrews 12:1 suggest we sign up for? What kind of race is this: short-term or long-term? Does anything come to mind you need to throw off this week?

2. Since we're trying to count steps and not calories, let's see what wisdom we can glean from a few verses. First, how could we have missed that our Lord was the first to count steps? (Someone needs to tell those folks at Fitbit.) Job 31:4 says, "Does he not see my ways and count my every step?"

a. From Psalm 121:1–5, where do we get help, and what happens to our feet? What other comforting tidbits do you find in this passage?

b. What does Habakkuk 3:19 reveal that our Sovereign Lord does for us? Why is this a confidence builder?

c. In Psalm 143:8 in the New Living Translation ("Let me hear of your unfailing love each morning, for I am trusting you. Show me where to walk, for I give myself to you"), what are we taught to ask for? Do you have a favorite phrase from this scripture? What blessing do you find from Deuteronomy 31:8?

3. "Walking in obedience" sounds rather dull. Forgive me, Lord. However, when we get out and walk with friends or family, in essence, we're walking not just for fellowship, but we're also taking care of our bodies, which is a form of obedience because we're instructed to care for our "temples" (2 Corinthians 6:19–20).

a. What three things are we asked to do in Deuteronomy 10:12? What extra component do you find in Deuteronomy 8:6?

b. What does King Solomon say in his blessing to the whole assembly of Israel in 1 Kings 8:57–58? We see that same phrase, but with another twist. What does "turning our hearts to him" mean to you? What is the blessing found in Psalm 128:1?

c. What are the three requirements mentioned in Micah 6:8? Share what that might look like toward people we meet each day, whether they're people we know or strangers we happen upon in a grocery store or coffee shop.

Sixth Stop: Mentoring (Friends from Tea: The Elizabethan Sisters)

1. Gatherings of the Elizabethan Sisters are always a learning experience. Though I shared from our sixth stop they're older

than I am, that's what I love about them because they're gold to me: They've lived a lot of life, they continually study God's Word, wanting to learn more, and they pour out grace, loving me unconditionally. Their experiences are a gold miner's dream. Get your pans out, and let's go diggin'.

    a. Liz Curtis Higgs blesses us with, "A single syllable, *grace* is God's word for *love*, expressed through divine forgiveness."[1] When was grace given to us, according to 2 Timothy 1:9? Is this because of how we're living our lives?

    b. Another blessing from my Elizabethan Sisters is they never judge me or look down on me. Whose job is it to judge, according to Deuteronomy 1:17? How does that take the pressure off all of us?

2. Another gift these sisters have blessed me with is countless opportunities to witness their love for God's Word. Whenever we get together, they share what they're currently learning. They're perpetual disciples.

    a. What do we learn about God's Word in Psalm 119:89? What does that mean to you?

    b. The Elizabethan Sisters often joke with each other, dubbing one of us "a Proverbs 31 woman." The next phrase that falls out of our mouths are, "Yeah, right." Verse 26 of Proverbs 31 really does describe my sisters. With what two things does this gal speak? How does that inspire you?

3. When Liz was writing *Embrace Grace,* many women wrote to her with their concerns about their faith. She includes many of their quotes in her book, answering them with grace.

One woman said something that particularly resonated with me, since I also came to faith later in my life. She said, "I always thought I was somehow less of a Christian because I came to know the Lord later in life and have a past. Now I know that

God can use even late bloomers to further His kingdom and help others."

To which Liz replies, "Bloom on, babe. Whatever experiences reside in our past or present, God can use them to mold a brighter future for others. And rest assured, there's no such thing as a less-than Christian."[2] What assurance for us late bloomers.

a. Read Hebrews 10:19–23, which is considered "A Call to Persevere in Faith." What gives us confidence and assurance? Why is that so hope-filled and, even better, guilt-free?

b. Whenever I see my sisters face a trial, their unswerving trust in God's sovereignty is inspirational. They cause me to say, "Well, if they can trust like that, maybe I need to do the same." Let's see how the prophet Habakkuk endured trials. Read Habakkuk 3:17–19 and find his solution. What does he call the Lord in verses 18 and 19? Write out a short prayer right now, praising Him regardless of your current circumstances. (Maybe try using that little word Habakkuk did: "yet.") Amen.

Seventh Stop: Praying (Friends from Prayer Groups: Prayer Warriors)

1. In her book *The Christian's Secret of a Happy Life*, Hannah Whitall Smith tells us, "What we need is to see that God's presence is a certain fact always, and that every act of our soul is done right before Him, and that a word spoken in prayer is really spoken to Him, as if our eyes could see Him and our hands could touch Him."[3]

Lessons learned from my prayer warriors are still far reaching. One thing I sometimes fail to remember is we must put on the full armor of God. I know where it is in the Bible, and, like getting dressed every day, I need to put that armor on. I forget there's a prowling lion out there seeking to devour us (1 Peter 5:8).

a. In order to avoid being shredded (that visual should remind us to armor up), list the six pieces of armor found in Ephesians 6:10–18. Don't miss what we're supposed to do and when, in verse 18. Would you also consider prayer a piece of armor? Which piece of armor is your favorite and why? Tomorrow, when you're combing your closet for something to wear, will you remember to put on the full armor of God? Maybe make a list of the armor to hang in your closet.

b. What's another way we can deftly demolish strongholds, thanks to 2 Corinthians 10:4–5? What does that look like?

c. What are we instructed to do in 1 Peter 4:7? What does it mean to be alert?

d. What's the good news found in 1 John 4:4? Let's read this together with victorious voices: "You, dear children, are from God and have overcome them, because the one who is in you is greater than the one who is in the world."

2. Sometimes in our distress, we're unable to think clearly.

a. What beautiful gift does the Holy Spirit offer us in these times, according to Romans 8:26? Why is this helpful or comforting?

b. Read Matthew 5:3 (The Message). Why are we blessed in this situation?

c. Which two "s" words are found in Isaiah 33:2? What encouragement do you find there? How often do we receive this?

Eighth Stop: Persevering (Befriending Prodigals)

1. Praying for prodigals is a tough assignment. Often frustrating, time seems to crawl at a snail's pace. While I still have a handful of prodigals I'm praying for, several have come home, returning

to their families and, more importantly, to the Lord. They are visual answers to prayer.

    a. How are we called to live now that we're out of darkness, according to Ephesians 5:8? How are we described?

    b. What's the benefit of walking in the light found in 1 John 1:7? What does that mean to you?

2. Our laundry is never completely done in this household. Yours?

    a. Read Psalm 51:7–15 (The Message). How does this idea of soaking and cleansing affect you? What does a "fresh start" or a "Genesis week" look like?

    b. In addition to cleansing, also found in Ezekiel 36:25–27, what two gifts are we given in verse 26?

3. My friend Jane helped me immensely once, when I was distraught over one of our boys. She said, "Go take a walk and praise the Lord." *What*? She added, "When you remember His goodness to you, it'll give you a fresh perspective on what to pray for." Great advice.

    a. Look at Psalm 77:11–15. How does this encourage you to continue moving forward?

    b. What beautiful picture does Psalm 85:10 leave us with?

    c. Olivia Sauder Mitchell showed us how a journal can help us remember several things: progress in praying for a prodigal and answered prayer, proving the faithfulness of the Lord, just for starters. What examples do Moses and Jethro offer us in Exodus 15:1–2 and 18:9–10? What does this look like in Ezra's life from Nehemiah 8:6?

Ninth Stop: Shopping and Cheering (Friends with Kin)

1. I'm obsessed with dish towels. Rankin' up there with shoes, purses, and devotionals, one can never have too many. My

favorite du jour says, "Remember, as far as everyone knows ... we are a *normal* family."

There never has been a "normal" family. If you don't believe me, crack your Bible open to Genesis and start with Adam. We all get to crash and burn, all too quickly, thanks to our sister, Eve. The only perfect person is our Lord, Jesus Christ. We praise you, Lord.

Nevertheless, we must strive to love our kinfolk. What two things does Romans 12:10 instruct us to do? How is it similar to the Golden Rule? (See Matthew 7:12.)

2. Leaving a legacy to our children and grandchildren is of utmost importance. Just from raising our boys, John and I've learned (sometimes the hard way) they're always watching. Yikes.

   a. Read Jeremiah 17:7–8. What is the challenge to us in the very last sentence? What's a way we can remind ourselves of this as each season changes ("season" can be used literally or figuratively)?

   b. We learned about the concept of being a balcony person in this chapter. As we cheer for our friends and family, who is the one who is always cheering for us, and how is He doing that? (See Zephaniah 3:17.)

   c. What two things are we told to do in 1 Thessalonians 5:11 (this is a "balcony person" verse if there ever was one)? What are some examples we can do this week in this endeavor?

3. The word *generation* is used over one hundred and fifty times in the Bible, depending on which translation you're using. We know any time a word is repeated in the Bible, it's significant.

   a. Let's look at Daniel 4:3. How long does God's kingdom and dominion last? What about His faithfulness in Psalm 100:4–5? What about His throne in Lamentations 5:19?

b. We talked about the act of remembering earlier. What is every generation supposed to do, similar to remembering, in Psalm 145:4–7?

Tenth Stop: Inviting (Friends with Practically Kin)

1. In an article in *Decision Magazine,* Billy Graham shared "the three invitations of Christ"[4]:
    a. "The first is an invitation to rest."[5] What does Matthew 11:28 say?
    b. "The second invitation is to discipleship."[6] What do Mark 1:17 and John 12:26 tell us?
    c. "The third invitation is to live in the realm of God."[7] What does that look like, according to David in Psalm 91:1?

2. What's a good reminder for us to be on the lookout for anyone who needs an invitation?
    a. What does Exodus 2:20 suggest?
    b. What happens in Job 1:4?

3. Winding down, heading heavenward, what does the Apostle Paul tell us is his only aim, described in Acts 20:24? What would this look like in our daily lives?
    a. As we age, we often hear, "Getting old is not for sissies." How can we keep from throwing in the towel, according to 2 Corinthians 4:16–18? What are we specifically told to do? What's the reward awaiting us, found in Job 19:25–27? As the NLT says, "I am overwhelmed." Yes, Lord.
    b. What does the faithful witness declare in Revelation 22:20? How are we to bookend our days until then, according to Psalm 113:3? And what's in store for us, per 2 Timothy 4:8?
    c. Close your time together, savoring Romans 8:31–39. What reassuring phrase is found in the second half of verse 31? What does that mean to you today? What is Christ doing for

us in verse 34? How would you rephrase verse 37? Finally, what is the best news ever, found in verses 38-39? I pray you're standing taller than when you began. This passage is powerful and equipping, and it gives us peace to sleep through the night, ready for another day.

May God bless you, precious sister-friend. Please pray about which Bible study you'll do next, since we've all learned we cope with circumstances much better when we keep our faces planted in God's Word.

I double-dog dare you to pray about inviting friends to do a Bible study together. Urge them on to utter an uncomfortable yes. They will thank you later.

On our tenth stop, we get to read Bob Russell's version of the gospel with one-syllable words. I ran across another way to see it, thanks to Ruth Chou Simons, a brave young mother of six boys. Share this invitation with your friends:

The gospel—the good news of Jesus Christ—is simply this:

The end to earning His favor	a beginning in surrender
The end to self-reliance	a beginning in forgiveness
The end to slavery to sin	a beginning in holiness
The end to condemnation	a beginning in freedom
The end to being good enough	a beginning in loving Christ more.[8]

The next time you meet up with a friend or your small group, may there be a bounty of butter for your muffins, croissants, rolls, scones, and biscuits. Amen.

Notes

Introduction

1. C. S. Lewis, *The Four Loves: An Exploration of the Nature of Love* (New York, NY: Houghton Mifflin Harcourt Publishing Company, 1960), 65.

First Stop: Discovering (Friends from the Book Club)

1. https://www.brainyquote.com/quotes/ernest_hemingway_152929
2. https://www.goodreads.com/quotes/2467-you-can-never-get-a-cup-of-tea-large-enough

Second Stop: Life-Giving (Friends Thanks to Our Kids: The Ya-Yas)

1. Deborah Ford, *The Grits (Girls Raised in the South) Guide to Life* (New York: The Penguin Group, a Plume Book, 1997), 246.
2. https://www.goodreads.com/work/quotes/3395562-letters-of-c-s-lewis-edited-with-a-memoir-by-w-h-lewis
3. Sophie Hudson, *Giddy Up, Eunice: Because Women Need Each Other* (Nashville, TN: B & H Publishing Group, 2016), 9.

Third Stop: Understanding (Friends from Bible Study)

1. https://www.goodreads.com/
   quotes/780508-a-party-without-cake-is-just-a-meeting
2. https://www.brainyquote.com/quotes/
   harry_emerson_fosdick_151765
3. https://www.brainyquote.com/quotes/a_a_milne_752340
4. https://www.goodreads.com/quotes/97518-friendship-is-the-
   only-cement-that-will-ever-hold-the

Fourth Stop: Laughing (Friends from Butter: The Butter Babes)

1. http://www.azquotes.com/quote/520053
2. Used with permission.
3. Charles Dickens, *A Christmas Carol* (London: Originally published by Chapman and Hall, 1843, http://www.open-bks.com, 2007 Open Books Electronic edition), 90.
4. Angela Thomas, *Choosing Joy: A 52-Week Devotional for Discovering True Happiness* (Nashville, TN: Howard Books, 2011), 67.
5. Konrad Lorenz, *On Aggression* (Orlando, FL: Harcourt Brace and Company, English translation, 1966), 284.
6. Shauna Niequist, *Bread and Wine: A Love Letter to Life Around the Table* (Grand Rapids, MI: 2013), 258.
7. Ford, *The Grits (Girls Raised in the South) Guide to Life*, xv.

Fifth Stop: Soul-Stretching (Friends from Walking)

1. http://biblereasons.com/walking-with-god/
2. Nancy Sleeth, "Why Is Honoring the Sabbath the Most Ignored Commandment?" in *Relevant Magazine* (March 15, 2017), http://www.relevantmagazine.com/article/why-is-honoring-the-sabbath-the-most-ignored-commandment/

3. http://www.azquotes.com/quote/524505

4. Paul David Tripp, *New Morning Mercies: A Daily Gospel Devotional* (Wheaton, IL: Crossway, 2014), entry from August 19.

5. Liz Curtis Higgs, *31 Verses to Write on Your Heart* (Colorado Springs, CO: Waterbrook Press, 2016), 112–113.

6. Ibid., 114.

7. https://www.gottman.com/blog/ the-grass-is-greener-where-you-water-it/

8. http://www.dailyinspirationalquotes.in/2016/06/ good-friends-help-find

Seventh Stop: Praying (Friends from Prayer Groups: Prayer Warriors)

1. Anne Graham Lotz, *The Daniel Prayer: Prayer That Moves Heaven and Changes Nations* (Grand Rapids, MI: Zondervan, 2016), 33.

2. Shauna Niequist, *Present Over Perfect: Leaving Behind Frantic for a Simpler, More Soulful Way of Living* (Grand Rapids, MI: Zondervan, 2016), 222.

Eighth Stop: Persevering (Befriending Prodigals)

1. Max Lucado, Twitter post, January 17, 2011, http://twitter.com/@MaxLucado.

2. Kristen Sauder, *Praying for Your Prodigal: A Journey through Luke* (Self-published, 2009), 5.

3. Ibid., 144.

4. Ken Boa, *Face to Face: Praying the Scriptures for Intimate Worship, Vol. 1* (Grand Rapids, MI: Zondervan, 1997), 176.

5. Mary Neal, *7 Lessons from Heaven: How Dying Taught Me to Live a Joy-Filled Life* (New York: Convergent, 2017), 249.

Ninth Stop: Shopping and Cheerig (Friends with Kin)

1. http://giantgag.net/im-a-shopaholic-on-the-road-to-recovery/
2. Joyce Landorf Heatherley, *Balcony People* (Georgetown, TX: Balcony Publishing, 2004), 17.
3. Ibid., 46.
4. https://www.goodreads.com/quotes/82798-what-wings-are-to-a-bird-and-sails-to-a

Tenth Stop: Inviting (Friends with Practically Kin)

1. http://www.brainyquote.com/quotes/david_whyte_523638
2. Rick Warren, *Daily Hope Devotional,* "You Need the Support of Your Spiritual Family," September 9, 2016, http://www.pastorrick.com
3. Sheldon Vanauken, *A Severe Mercy, Davy's Edition* (San Francisco: Harper and Row, 1977), 230.

Discussion Questions for Book Clubs or Small Groups

1. Bob Merritt, *Get Wise: Make Great Decisions Every Day* (Grand Rapids, MI: Baker Books, 2014), 118–119.
2. https://www.brainyquote.com/quotes/claude_chabrol_462234

Discussion Questions for Bible Study

1. Liz Curtis Higgs, *Embrace Grace: Welcome to the Forgiven Life* (Colorado Springs, CO: Waterbrook Press, 2006), 7.
2. Ibid., p. 137.
3. Hanna Whitall Smith, *The Christians' Secret of a Happy Life* (Chicago: Moody Publishers, 2009, originally published in 1883 by Fleming H. Revell), 71.

4. Billy Graham, *Decision Magazine,* "The Three Invitations of Christ" (Charlotte, NC: The Billy Graham Evangelical Association).

5. Ibid.

6. Ibid.

7. Ibid.

8. Ruth Chou Simons, *Gracelaced: Discovering Timeless Truths through Seasons of the Heart* (Eugene, OR: Harvest House, 2017), 221.

Contributors

Nancy Aguiar, author of *Five Drops: Stories of Faith, Family, and Fun*, is a Bible teacher who loves people. She currently works in the health care industry and is happily married to Ron, founder and CEO of Oasis Safety. They live in Louisville and have a son, a daughter, and a grandson.

Denita Arnold is a writer, speaker, teaching leader, mentor, and disciple maker. She serves as a leader in women's ministry at Southeast Christian Church in Louisville. Denita is president of A Woman Like You Foundation, started by her late sister. She and her husband Mike are Louisville natives; they have three adult and two teenage children and one grandchild. Denita loves family, ministry, and traveling.

Sarah Grace Bloyd is a worship leader and writer with a big voice, big dreams, and an even bigger heart for serving Jesus and loving people. She holds a bachelor's of arts from Asbury University, where she pursued a major in worship arts with an emphasis in music. Currently residing in Louisville, Sarah Grace is the Elementary Secretary at Christian Academy of Louisville, and she co-leads the fifth grade praise team there. She spends her free time writing poetry and Christian nonfiction that she hopes to publish.

Carol Bonura was born in New Orleans and now resides in Louisville. She graduated with a bachelor's of arts degree in art history from the University of Louisville. She's been married to her husband, Joe, for more than fifty years. They have three children and sixteen grandchildren. In 2016, she published her first book, *Our God Is a Big God: Personal Stories of Those Touched by the Bigness of God.*

Doris Bridgeman, of Louisville, is a former Bible Study Fellowship leader as well as being a former leader in women's ministry at Southeast Christian Church. Currently, she's proud to be a member of the Abbies, a ladies' in-home Bible study group. She and her husband, Ulysses, are parents to three married children, who have blessed them with three grandchildren.

Jane Chilton lives in Louisville, where she is a wife, mother, grandmother, Bible teacher, mentor, novel reader, lunch-with-her-girlfriends aficionado, and a friend of Jesus.

Ginny Crowe finds great joy in leading Bible studies for women. She and her husband, Greg, live in Carmel, Indiana, and have two grown children who are married to two lovely spouses. She enjoys chocolate, tea, spy novels, and, of course, studying the Word of God.

Kathy Hampton Daniels was married to Joe, the love of her life, for almost thirty-two years, until he passed away from kidney cancer. They have two children, Matthew (married to Jenny) and Kaitlin (married to Lucas), plus seven "grand darlin's," as she calls them. Being a Realtor and a very busy grandmother keeps Kathy traveling in all directions. She facilitated a coaches' wives Bible study for many years in Columbus, Ohio, where she lives. She's now in a neighborhood Bible study, remains an avid reader, a chocoholic, and loves to cook great quantities for friends and family.

Jamie Lynn Dorr grew up in Kentucky, but after moving to Alabama for college, she became a true Southern girl, with a double name to boot. She met her husband, Jake, at the University of Alabama. She became smitten with him for his "adorable smile, love of skipping class, and serving God on Sundays." Jake and Jamie have been married for four years, have two precious children in heaven, and are expecting two children in the fall of 2018 (Jamie just delivered Selah James on 9/2/18. Her name means "to pause and praise." Amen!) one through the miracle of pregnancy and one through the miracle of adoption. They've planted roots in Mississippi, where they hope to grow their family. Jamie loves to nurture her house plants and prays to finally get rid of the lizard that keeps finding itself at home in their house. She leads a small group of college girls at Ole Miss and is a member of Pinelake Church.

Laura Leavell Fincher is the agency/community relationship manager at the Food Bank of North Alabama. Originally hailing from Louisville, Laura attended the University of Kentucky, where she studied agricultural economics (B.S.) and international relations (M.A.). Laura now lives in Tanner, Alabama, where she assists her husband, Stephen, as he pastors Tanner United Methodist Church. In her free time, Laura enjoys riding horses, gardening (dahlias especially), book club, and doting on her three cats. She and Stephen are expecting their first child in February of 2019.

Pat Hall is a retired school library media specialist who lives in Louisville. She loves the Lord, her church, Bible studies, reading, traveling, being with friends, and family visits. She has one sister, three nieces, and an abundance of great-nieces and great-nephews. Her cat child, Wilbur, allows her to live in their house.

Betsy Heady leads a coed Bible study with her husband, David. She's a mother to two married daughters and one daughter-in-law. She's a grandmother to five granddaughters and one grandson. She's a confessed Bible study and reading addict.

Liz Curtis Higgs has one goal: to help women embrace the grace of God with joy and abandon. Her messages are biblical, encouraging, down-to-earth, and profoundly funny, helping sisters and seekers experience the depth of God's love. Liz is the author of thirty-seven books, with 4.6 million copies in print, including her nonfiction bestsellers, *Bad Girls of the Bible, The Girl's Still Got It*, and *The Women of Christmas*. Liz has spoken for Women of Faith, Women of Joy, Extraordinary Women, and eighteen hundred other Christian conferences in all fifty states and fifteen foreign countries. Louisville is home for Liz, her husband, Bill, and their grown children, Matt, Lilly, and daughter-in-love, Beth. Liz admits she's a lame housekeeper, a marginal cook, and a mediocre gardener, but she loves studying and teaching God's Word. Look for her monthly Bible study at LizCurtisHiggs.com.

Marte Hoagland is a women's outreach Bible study leader of her neighborhood church. She and her husband, Bill, are the parents of a married daughter and son, and are grandparents to three granddaughters. A growing love and concern for women in crisis pregnancies has moved her to begin counseling for life through A Woman's Choice Resource Center in Louisville.

Becky Aguiar Jarrell is a homemaker with fifteen years of experience in marketing and public relations. She, along with her son, Silas, live in Atlanta. They have two dogs, Eleanor and Sullivan, and spend their days exploring all Atlanta has to offer. When she has a rare spare moment, she tries to finish reading her book for her monthly neighborhood book club.

Elizabeth Jeffries is married to Stephen and is oftentimes referred to as a marketplace minister. With God's Word as her guide, she works with executives who want to develop their leadership skills and those of their team. An award-winning professional speaker and author of several books, Elizabeth presents keynote speeches, facilitates learning retreats, and coaches business leaders in the way of a servant-leader. Elizabeth is an avid traveler, reader, learner, and lover of Italy and all things Italian.

Bonnie Johnson holds an MFA degree from Spalding University. She writes fiction and nonfiction books, leads writing workshops for Shape and Flow Studio, and is an adjunct professor at Bellarmine University in Louisville, where she teaches composition, literature, and creative writing. She is a devoted foodie who relishes gatherings with friends and family, reading, art, holidays, decorating, gardening, and travel. She lives in Louisville with Steve, her "baby daddy" and husband of fifty years. They have one son and two daughters, who are married, and have six grandchildren. Bonnie's domestic skills include making bows, cheesecake, and biscotti; her domestic fails include dusting and floor-sweeping.

Diane Kennedy is married to Mark, and they live in Louisville. They have three grown, married children. She's a doting grandmother to three adorable grandchildren (so far). She and Mark are active in their church and community. Diane is a voracious reader.

Katie Kirtley was born and raised in Birmingham, Alabama. She attended Washington and Lee University and earned an MA in art history at the Courtauld Institute of Art in London. She has worked in membership and development at several art museums, including the Phillips Collection and the Smithsonian Freer and Sackler Galleries in Washington DC. She currently lives in Atlanta with her husband, Chris, and their three children.

Olivia Kirtley (yes, she's the above Katie's mother-in-love) is a former chairman and president of the International Federation of Accountants (IFAC), representing the global accountancy profession, with members in 130 countries. She has traveled extensively for business and missions, having the privilege of working with people across six continents from multiple cultures and backgrounds. She is currently a director of public companies in the United States and the UK. She's married to Louis, her childhood best friend. They have three sons and two daughters-in-law who are the light of their world (as are their five grandchildren, of course).

Sherry Leavell has been in financial services for thirty-six years and has been married to her husband, Bill, for thirty years. They have two married daughters and two grandchildren, with another one due in 2019. Sherry and Bill live in Louisville. Sherry enjoys worshipping and serving at Southeast Christian Church.

Olivia Sauder Mitchell is currently in grad school at Southern Seminary, working on a degree in biblical counseling. She and her husband, Matthew, both work in full-time ministry and are foster parents in Louisville.

Gwen Paten was married to Mike for twenty-one years before he passed away from cancer. She continues to live in Louisville and enjoys spending time with her children and grandchildren. Gwen volunteered and was on staff at Southeast Christian Church in women's ministry for twenty-two years. She is still involved in Bible study and small group fellowship with many women she ministered to through those years.

Becky Pippert is recognized internationally as an author, speaker, evangelist, and the founder of Becky Pippert Ministries, a global evangelism ministry. Becky and her husband, Dick, have ministered extensively on all six continents and lived and ministered in the UK and Europe for seven years. Becky is the author of eleven books. She and Dick are parents to four adult children, and they have four grandchildren. When not traveling (or hugging and reading books to their grandchildren), they reside in Holland, Michigan.

Lynn Reece is a girl raised in the South (GRITS) and proud of it. Much of her adult life was influenced by growing up in a small town in Georgia. Her life was radically changed after her minister husband, who suffered from severe depression, took his life. Lynn feels God turned sorrow into joy, as she's been able to help countless women on their spiritual journeys. She spent fourteen years leading the women at Southeast Christian Church and now leads women's community Bible studies in Louisville. She also volunteers at a recovery house for women recently out of prison. She and her husband, Tom, enjoy spending time with their five-year-old granddaughter. Lynn's goal in life is to share God's Word with as many women as she can while making an impact for Christ.

Luly Reinhardt has been happily married to her husband, Greg, since 1980. She's the mother of an adopted daughter and has one granddaughter. She serves in both community and church-related ministries. She's a residential Realtor in Louisville and treasures her girlfriends, with whom she loves to organize and socialize.

Judy Russell is the wife of Bob, a retired minister. They live in Louisville and have two married sons: Rusty, who's the lead pastor at New Day Christian Church in Port Charlotte, Florida, and Phil, who's a lieutenant with the Louisville Metro Police Department. Judy and Bob have seven grandchildren: five boys and two girls. Their oldest grandson is married and in ministry. Judy loves entertaining, photography, scrapbooking, and Bible studies. She also loves being with family and friends. She's presently Bob's travel coordinator and helps him with Bob Russell Ministries.

Nancy Sleeth is the author of *Almost Amish* and cofounder of Blessed Earth. Her husband, Matthew, and their grown children all serve Jesus as writers, pastors, and medical missionaries. *Christianity Today* and *Newsweek* have recognized Nancy among the fifty evangelical women most shaping culture and the church today, but her favorite title is "Nana" to Hannah, her granddaughter.

Cassie Soete and her late husband, George, started the Marriage Mentoring Ministry at Southeast Christian Church over twenty-five years ago. She spends most of her time mentoring troubled marriages and giving God the glory. She's a mother of five daughters and one son. She's nana to thirteen grandchildren. When she's not with family or mentoring, she loves to spend time in her garden.

Aletia Thompson passionately loves the Lord and His Word. She is appreciative of her many blessings, which include a marriage to Frank of thirty-plus years, her amazing two daughters, Chelsea and Lindsey-Taylor, son-in-loves Jonathan and Woody, and being "Memo" to her precious cherished grandchildren, Ava and Silas (with more on the way). Aletia's spiritual life and walk with the Lord have been enhanced and blessed by the various Bible study groups she has participated in, along with her twenty-plus years of being a member of Southeast Christian Church.

Nancy Tinnell is an associate pastor at Middletown United Methodist Church in Louisville, where she leads Branches women's ministry and discipleship ministries. She is married with three children and three grandchildren. She teaches Image Bible Study, a community study for women, and helps with monthly Branches book club meetings. In addition to Christian fiction and classic fiction, Nancy loves to read and write poetry.

Pam Van Arsdall is a retired professor from the University of Kentucky. She leads the ministry called A Million God Stories (www.amilliongodstories.com). Pam lives in Nicholasville, Kentucky, with her husband, Alan. They have three children and one son-in-law. Pam loves to read, cook, and garden.

Reggie Willinger and her husband, Andy, live in Louisville and are the parents of six children. They have four sons, a daughter-in-law, two daughters, and two granddaughters. Reggie loves to read, attend Bible study with the Abbies, and travel with her family.

Mary Young is a retired elementary schoolteacher. Mary's life revolves around her family. She's married to Michael and is the mother to Lacy. Lacy's an Assistant Principal and is married to Dale. Mary is a stepmother to Josh and Travis. Travis and his wife, Alli, recently blessed Mary and Michael with a granddaughter, Riley. Mary enjoys weekly Bible study, time with friends, walking, swimming, traveling, and reading.

Lisa Zaring is a placement director at Sullivan University, where she helps families from all over the United States find a perfect nanny match from the Professional Nanny Program. With that program coming to an end, she's looking for her next chapter. Lover of all food sans gluten and dairy, she's constantly looking for a perfect bread. Flowers and all things making up a pretty home are her passion. Grace-filled books make her heart sing, as well as her loving husband, Guthrie. They have a son, two daughters, and a handsome son-in-law, and are expecting their first grandchild in February of 2019. Their house is rounded out by a rescue dog named Lilly, a wandering escape artist, and her son's cat, Skimbleshanks.

Where Can You Find My Friends?

(Contributors to this book and on my website, www.
elizabethhoagland.com, are found in *Pass the Butter: A Collection
of Recipes.*)

Nancy Aguiar (Nancy the Hugging Evangelist): Stops 1 and 4
Denita Arnold: Stop 10
Fay Bloyd: Stop 4
Sarah Grace Bloyd: Stop 10
Carol Bonura: Stop 6
Doris Bridgeman: Stop 7
Susan Bugh: Stop 2; Decadent Chocolate Topped Cheesecake
    Bars (website)
Thelma Button: Lemon Apricot Cake, Stop 10
Diane Carter: Penne Pasta with Italian Sausage and Bacon, and
    Delish and Easy Spring Salad (website)
Jane Chilton: Stop 7; Motivation-for-getting-to-Bible-study
    Biscuits, Stop 3; Pound Cake (website)
Jayne Combs: Stop 2
Ginny Crowe: Stop 6
Kathy Hampton Daniels and Matthew Joseph Daniels: Stop
    2; Joe D.'s Favorite Italian Dish: Homemade Meatballs and
    Spaghetti Sauce, Stop 6
Jamie Lynn Dorr: Stop 10

Valerie Ducas: Funeral Fruit Salad (website)

Laura Leavell Fincher: Stop 5

Beverly Fleece: Hearty Fight-over-It Sausage Appetizer, Stop 2

Pat Hall: Stop 1; Not-Too-Spicy Taco Soup, Stop 1

Bill Hawkins (from the Bluebird Café in Stanford, Kentucky): Spinach Salad with Honey Vinaigrette, Stop 6

Betsy Heady: Stop 3; Gluten-Free Pumpkin Bars (website)

Liz Curtis Higgs: Foreword; Stop 6; Bloom-and-Shine Peach and Blueberry Puff Pancakes, and Glazed Honeymoon Muffins (website)

John G. Hoagland, Jr.: Sketches for each stop

Marte Hoagland: Stop 9

Ron Holt: Foolproof Marinade for Grilled Salmon, Stop 8

Becky Aguiar Jarrell: Stop 10

Elizabeth Jeffries: Stop 6; Italian Crème Cake (website)

Bonnie Omer Johnson: Stop 4; Sour Cream Muffins and Not-Your-Average Rice Krispie Treats (website)

Diane Kennedy: Stop 1; White Lightning Chili (website)

Katie Kirtley: Great-for-Gifts or Snacking Granola (website)

Olivia Kirtley: Stop 3; Easiest Banana Bread, Vegan Too! (website)

Sherry Leavell: Stop 5

Mary Lewis: Cracked Up Pot Roast in a Crock-Pot, Stop 7; Crack Tomatoes (website)

Olivia Sauder Mitchell: Stop 8

Meredith Myers: Homemade Fudge Cake and Chocolate Sauce, Stop 10

Gwen Paten: Stop 3; Chocolate Chip and Walnut Pie (website)

Becky Pippert: Stop 7

Lynn Reece: Stop 3; To-Die-For Cheese Grits (website)

Luly Reinhardt: Stop 1

Bob Russell: Stop 10

Judy Russell: Stop 4

Denise Seiz: Stop 2; Grilled Salmon Rub, Stop 8

Nancy Sleeth (Almost Amish Nancy): Stop 5; Chocolate Nemesis, Stop 5; Artisan Flaxseed Bread (website)

Cassie Soete: Stop 8

Nancy Tarrant (Owner of the Cheddar Box in St. Matthews, Louisville, Kentucky): Hot Brown Casserole for the Soul, Stop 4

Aletia Thompson: Stop 9; Chicken Tetrazzini (website)

Nancy Tinnell (Guardian Angel Nancy): Stop 1; Coffee Ice Cream Dessert (website)

Pam Van Arsdall: Stop 9; Gluten-Free Chocolate Chip Pecan Pie (website)

Reggie Willinger: Stop 7; Chocolate Chip and Walnut Pie (website)

Matt Weber (Chef from the Uptown Café, Louisville, Kentucky): Stuffed Mushroom Caps Appetizer, Stop 2

Mary Young: Stop 5

Lisa Zaring: Stop 10

With Gratitude

First and foremost, I must thank our gracious heavenly Father. He helped me put this book together. There's no way I could've done it without Him and the friends He's blessed me with. What a project, Lord. Continued thanks for your mercy, grace, and rescue. Apologies for being a slow study.

I cannot begin to thank my fabulous family for putting up with me during the writing of this book: My beloved husband, John, and our precious children John Jr., Diana, Gordy, Lauren, Woody and LT, each so unique in so many ways, faithfully praying me to the finish line.

During this writing process, we also got to welcome into the world our first grandchild, our granddaughter, Claire Elizabeth. While she's a gift to us all, this was a bit of a juggling act, as I wanted to hold her but had to work at the computer. We did a little of both. May we all teach her about Jesus and leave her a legacy of faith.

It wasn't from me, but from our baby Woody's first Sunday school teacher, who taught him scripture at the ripe age of nearly two. He came home talking on a play telephone, shaking his head, saying, "No, He is not here. He is rizzzzen" (Matthew 28:6). Oh, may we seize these moments!

Huge thanks go to our firstborn, John Jr., who created the sketches at the beginning of each stop. (One of his many talents.) He depicted exactly what I wanted you, the reader, to see as a picture of something important to my friends you met on those stops.

Gargantuan thanks go to my two dear, dear sister-friends who came up with the idea for this book in two different cities, in two different weeks, unbeknownst to one another, suggesting the exact same idea. I took that as a divine suggestion. These gals are to be commended for their patience and the sweat equity they've poured over me, lo these past many months: Liz Curtis Higgs and Nancy Sleeth.

Mega thanks go to my new friend and angel-in-disguise editor, Becky Nesbitt. She thinks of things that would never have crossed my mind; a huge portion of the credit goes to her. She dubs herself "a midwife to the author." Amen.

Not having to deal with the book's formatting frenzy was a gift from my blog guru, Kelly McDonald. She speaks computer, while I often fear it. She sweeps up after me, tying everything up into a tidy knot. Honestly, she's another guardian angel of mine (recommended by Guardian Angel Nancy, no less.).

Colossal thanks go to all my sister-friends you met in this book and any I accidentally forgot to mention. Many of my growing up and high school buddies from Lexington, who I've reconnected with recently, could fill another page. I wouldn't be where I am today, nor have learned the things they taught me, without the Lord crossing our paths. We praise you, Lord.

Don't miss photos of all these wonderful, beautiful sister-friends on my website (www.elizabethhoagland.com).